Crystallization-Study
of
Acts

Volume One

Witness Lee

The Holy Word for Morning Revival

Living Stream Ministry
Anaheim, CA • www.lsm.org

© 2009 Living Stream Ministry

First Edition, January 2009.

ISBN 978-0-7363-3917-9

Published by

Living Stream Ministry
2431 W. La Palma Ave., Anaheim, CA 92801 U.S.A.
P. O. Box 2121, Anaheim, CA 92814 U.S.A.

Printed in the United States of America

09 10 11 12 13 14 / 9 8 7 6 5 4 3 2 1

Contents

Preface

1. This book is intended as an aid to believers in developing a daily time of morning revival with the Lord in His word. At the same time, it provides a limited review of the winter training on the "Crystallization-study of Acts" held in Anaheim, California, December 22-27, 2008. Through intimate contact with the Lord in His word, the believers can be constituted with life and truth and thereby equipped to prophesy in the meetings of the church unto the building up of the Body of Christ.

2. The entire content of this book is taken from the *Crystallization-study Outlines: Acts,* the text and footnotes of the Recovery Version of the Bible, selections from the writings of Witness Lee and Watchman Nee, and *Hymns,* all of which are published by Living Stream Ministry.

3. The book is divided into weeks. One training message is covered per week. Each week presents first the message outline, followed by six daily portions, a hymn, and then some space for writing. The training outline has been divided into days, corresponding to the six daily portions. Each daily portion covers certain points and begins with a section entitled "Morning Nourishment." This section contains selected verses and a short reading that can provide rich spiritual nourishment through intimate fellowship with the Lord. The "Morning Nourishment" is followed by a section entitled "Today's Reading," a longer portion of ministry related to the day's main points. Each day's portion concludes with a short list of references for further reading and some space for the saints to make notes concerning their spiritual inspiration, enlightenment, and enjoyment to serve as a reminder of what they have received of the Lord that day.

4. The space provided at the end of each week is for composing a short prophecy. This prophecy can be composed by considering all of our daily notes, the "harvest" of our inspirations during the week, and preparing a main point

with some sub-points to be spoken in the church meetings for the organic building up of the Body of Christ.

5. Following the last week in this volume, we have provided reading schedules for both the Old and New Testaments in the Recovery Version with footnotes. These schedules are arranged so that one can read through both the Old and New Testaments of the Recovery Version with footnotes in two years.

6. As a practical aid to the saints' feeding on the Word throughout the day, we have provided verse cards at the end of the volume, which correspond to each day's Scripture reading. These may be cut out and carried along as a source of spiritual enlightenment and nourishment in the saints' daily lives.

7. The *Crystallization-study Outlines* were compiled by Living Stream Ministry from the writings of Witness Lee and Watchman Nee. The outlines, footnotes, and references in the Recovery Version of the Bible are by Witness Lee. All of the other references cited in this publication are from the published ministry of Witness Lee and Watchman Nee.

Winter Training

(December 22-27, 2008)

CRYSTALLIZATION-STUDY
OF
ACTS

Banners:

To carry out His heavenly ministry
for the propagating of Himself,
the ascended Christ
uses a body of His witnesses,
who bear a living testimony of the
incarnated, crucified, resurrected,
and ascended Christ.

We must receive the Lord's mercy
to keep ourselves in the flow of the age,
the one flow of the Lord's work,
for the spreading and building up
of the church.

We need to see
the vision of God's eternal economy
and have a dispensational transfer
so that we may live a life
fully according to and for
God's New Testament economy.

The continuation of the book of Acts
is the corporate continuation of Christ
with the corporate living
of the perfected God-men
as the reality of the Body of Christ.

The Intrinsic Significance of the Book of Acts
and
Witnesses of the Resurrection of the Lord Jesus

Scripture Reading: Acts 1:8-11, 14, 22; 2:24, 32-33; 4:33; 10:39-40; 26:16

Day 1   **I. We need to see the intrinsic significance of the book of Acts:**

A. The Acts of the Apostles is a book without an ending; this book is still being continued, because Acts is a record of the work of God, who is always advancing and never stops (28:30-31).

B. In the book of Acts the disciples are the continuation of the Lord Jesus (1:14):

1. The Lord brought the disciples with Him into His death and resurrection; this means that they passed through the same processes through which the Lord Jesus passed (Rom. 6:6; Eph. 2:5-6).

2. By passing through the Lord's death and resurrection, His disciples became His continuation; this continuation is unveiled in the book of Acts (1:14).

3. By replacing the disciples with Himself, the Lord Jesus made them His reproduction; therefore, they became His increase, development, enlargement, and continuation— the church as His extension in time and His spread in space (John 12:24; 14:19; Gal. 2:20; Acts 8:1; 9:31).

Day 2   C. The book of Acts is a record of a group of people who are resurrected and ascended with Christ, having Christ within them as their life and Christ upon them as their power and authority; they live by the Triune God within them as their life, and they act by the Triune God upon them as their strength, power, and authority (John 20:22; Luke 24:49; Acts 1:8).

D. Acts is a record of a group of people who act and work in the Body, through the Body, and for the Body (v. 14; 13:1-4a):

 1. Acts reveals the move and activity of the Body, not of individual actions unrelated to the Body (8:1-17).

 2. Acts contains a beautiful picture of the one accord in the activities and work of the believers who moved in the Body, through the Body, and for the Body (2:44-47; 4:24, 32; 13:1-4a; 16:1-5).

E. The book of Acts shows us the divine stream, the unique flow; there is only one stream, one current, of the flow (Gen. 2:8-12; Rev. 22:1-2; Acts 2:33).

Day 3 F. In Acts there is a group of people who know the meaning of resurrection and ascension, who live by Christ as their life, who act by Christ as their power and authority, and who realize that they are the Body and act in the Body and for the Body in the one divine stream; this is the intrinsic significance of the book of Acts (John 20:22; Acts 1:8-11, 14; 2:1-4, 24, 32-33; 4:33).

II. **The apostles and disciples were witnesses of the resurrection of the Lord Jesus (1:8, 22; 2:24, 32; 4:2, 33; 10:39-40; 17:3, 18; 23:11; 24:14-15):**

A. To carry out His heavenly ministry for the propagating of Himself so that the kingdom of God might be established for the building up of the churches as His fullness, the ascended Christ uses not a group of preachers trained by man's teaching to do a preaching work but a body of His witnesses, who bear a living testimony of the incarnated, crucified, resurrected, and ascended Christ (1:8):

 1. The apostles and disciples were the Lord's witnesses (lit., martyrs); all the apostles and disciples in Acts were His martyrs, His witnesses, of this kind (v. 8; 2:40; 10:39-41; 22:20; 23:11; 26:16).

    2. In His ascension the Lord carries out His ministry in the heavens through these martyrs, in His resurrection life and with His ascension power and authority, as recorded in Acts, to spread Himself as the development of the kingdom of God from Jerusalem unto the uttermost part of the earth (1:8).

    3. Testifying requires experiences of seeing and enjoyment concerning the Lord or spiritual things; it is different from merely teaching (2:40).

    4. Paul was appointed as a minister and a witness (26:16):

       a. A minister is for the ministry; a witness, for the testimony.

       b. The ministry is related mainly to the work, to what a minister does; a testimony is related to the person, to what a witness is.

Day 4

    5. Luke's narration, as an account of the Lord's move on earth, stresses not doctrine but the testimony of the Lord's witnesses; hence, in his narration there are no details related to doctrine; rather, there are details regarding the things that happened to His witnesses, in order to portray the testimonies of their lives (27:21; 1:8).

B. The Lord's resurrection was the focus of the apostles' testimony (1:22; 2:32; 3:13, 15, 26; 10:39-40; 13:33; 17:3, 18):

    1. The resurrection of the Lord Jesus points back to His incarnation, humanity, human living on the earth, and God-ordained death, and His resurrection points forward to His ascension, ministry and administration in heaven, and coming back (2:23; 1:9-11).

    2. The Lord is both God and resurrection, possessing the indestructible life (John 1:1; 11:25; Heb. 7:16; Acts 2:24):

    a. Since He is such an ever-living One, death is not able to hold Him.

    b. He delivered Himself to death, but death had no way to detain Him; rather, death was defeated by Him, and He rose up from it (Rev. 1:18).

3. The apostles were witnesses of the resurrected Christ, not only in word but also by their life and action, especially bearing witness of His resurrection; bearing witness of Christ's resurrection is the crucial point, the focus, in carrying out God's New Testament economy (Acts 2:32; 4:33; 10:39-40; 17:3).

Day 5

4. God glorified His Servant Jesus through His resurrection and in His ascension (Luke 24:46; Eph. 1:20-22; Phil. 2:9-11; Acts 3:13, 15, 26; 4:10, 33; 5:30-31).

5. Resurrection was a birth to the man Jesus (13:33):

    a. He was begotten by God in His resurrection to be the firstborn Son of God among many brothers (Rom. 1:3-4; 8:29).

    b. He was the only begotten Son of God from eternity; after incarnation, through resurrection He was begotten by God in His humanity to be God's firstborn Son (John 1:18; 3:16; Rom. 8:29; Heb. 1:6).

6. We need to know the power of Christ's resurrection (Eph. 1:19; Phil. 3:10):

    a. In His resurrection the Lord Jesus broke through all barriers, even the greatest barrier of all—death (Rom. 6:9; Rev. 1:18; Eph. 1:19-20):

        1) Death is the greatest limitation, but resurrection has conquered death; thus, resurrection is the greatest power of all (Acts 2:24).

        2) In His resurrection the Lord Jesus transcended time and space (Eph. 1:19-21).

b. The power of resurrection, and even resurrection itself, is now in the life-giving
Spirit, the Spirit of Jesus Christ (1 Cor.
15:45b; Phil. 1:19).

c. Ephesians 1:19-20 speaks of the surpassing greatness of God's power toward
us who believe; this is the resurrection
power manifested by God in Christ
through His raising Him from the dead.

d. The church is the place where God dem-
onstrates the operation of the might of
His strength, according to the power which
He caused to operate in Christ (vv. 19-20):

  1) The church is the same as the resurrected Christ not only in nature but
  also in power (vv. 19-22; 3:16; 6:10).

  2) The church is the depository and
  storehouse of the power of Christ's
  resurrection (Phil. 3:10).

  3) The church is the same as Christ in
  resurrection and should be as unlimited and victorious as Christ is (Eph.
  1:19-23).

  4) If two or three see this revelation,
  touch the power of Christ's resurrection, and pray in one accord, they will
  shake the ends of the earth (Matt.
  18:18-20; Acts 1:14; 4:23-33).

Morning Nourishment

Acts And [Paul] remained two whole years in *his* own
28:30-31 rented dwelling and welcomed all those who came
to him, proclaiming the kingdom of God and teaching the things concerning the Lord Jesus Christ
with all boldness, unhindered.

John Truly, truly, I say to you, Unless the grain of wheat
12:24 falls into the ground and dies, it abides alone; but if it
dies, it bears much fruit.

The book of Acts does not have an ending. After chapter
twenty-eight, many of God's vessels are still carrying on with His
work. His work is continuing and has not stopped. Everything
was not over after Paul worked in Rome for two years. Paul lived
in Rome and was later martyred. None of these things are
recorded in the book of Acts. Peter, Paul, and John are three
important persons, yet none of their endings were recorded. How
can we say that the book of Acts has ended? God's testimony can
never be finished. We could say the same thing even if there was a
twenty-ninth chapter, or a thirtieth chapter, or even a hundredth
chapter. If one wanted to write more, new things could always be
added. This is why Acts stops at chapter twenty-eight. Although
the written record no longer continued,...God's work has been
going on. The work in the first century was not the peak. For four
thousand years, God has been working....His work will go on
until the kingdom and even until the new heaven and the new
earth. God is always advancing; He never stops. (*The Collected
Works of Watchman Nee,* vol. 37, p. 122)

Today's Reading

[In the Gospel of Mark we see] that the Lord's disciples followed Him from the beginning of His ministry. The Lord brought
them on step by step wherever He went. He even brought them
with Him into His death and resurrection. This means that the
disciples passed through the processes through which the Slave-
Savior passed.

By passing through the Lord's death and resurrection His

disciples became His continuation. This continuation is unveiled in the book of Acts....In chapter one of Acts the disciples are the Lord's continuation, following Him to live a life according to God's New Testament economy.

In the second chapter of Acts, the power from on high came upon the disciples. As a result, they became the increase, development, enlargement, and continuation of the Lord Jesus. He had brought them through His death and His resurrection, and He had wrought Himself into them. As a result, they were replaced by the Lord and saturated with Him. In this way they became His increase and continuation.

What kind of life did the one hundred twenty live in the book of Acts? They lived a life that was fully according to God's New Testament economy. They did not live a life of culture or religion. Neither did they live a life of ethics, morality, philosophy, or improvement of character. Just as the Lord Jesus lived absolutely according to and for God's New Testament economy, so the one hundred twenty in Acts lived the same way. (*Life-study of Mark*, pp. 581, 537)

The infinite life of Christ with its infinite power has entered into us. Just as He is, so also are we. Just as He has the life of God, so we also have the life of God. Moreover, the life that is in us is the power of God....Strictly speaking,...Acts is...the biography of Jesus. The four Gospels are the biographies of Jesus as an individual, while Acts is the biography of Jesus in the disciples. Hence, there is not only one Jesus in Acts. The disciples of the Lord became the church as His extension in time and His spread in space. After two thousand years of extending and spreading, this Jesus is now in the United States and in China at the same time; He is in the East and in the West simultaneously. This is the purpose God intends to accomplish. The reason the Lord Jesus had to die and be raised was so that He could enter into man to be man's life for His spread and extension. (*The Crucified Christ*, p. 41)

Further Reading: The Collected Works of Watchman Nee, vol. 37, ch. 20; Life-study of Mark, msgs. 63, 69

Enlightenment and inspiration: _____

_____

_____

_____

Morning Nourishment

Luke   And behold, I send forth the promise of My Father
24:49   upon you; but as for you, stay in the city until you put
          on power from on high.
Acts   These all continued steadfastly with one accord in
1:14   prayer...
2:46   And day by day, continuing steadfastly with one
          accord in the temple and breaking bread from house
          to house...

The book of Acts is a record of a group of people who are resurrected and ascended with Christ, having Christ within them as their life and Christ upon them as their power and authority. They live not by themselves but by Christ as life. They forget about their own life and deny themselves. Moreover, they walk, act, and work not by their own strength, their own way, or their own method but by Christ as their power, their way, and their method. This Christ who is now their method, way, and power is the very Holy Spirit who came down upon them. In other words, they live by the Triune God within them as their life, and they act by the Triune God upon them as their strength, their way, and their method.

In the Holy Spirit within us we have the reality of resurrection, and with the Holy Spirit upon us we have the reality of ascension. Therefore, within us we have life, and upon us we have authority and power. (*A General Sketch of the New Testament in the Light of Christ and the Church, Part 1: The Gospels and the Acts,* pp. 87-89)

Today's Reading

The entire record of the book of Acts also shows us a group of people who always acted as the Body. From the very first chapter neither Peter, John, nor those one hundred twenty acted individually. Rather, all the actions of this group of people were the actions of the one Body. The one hundred twenty prayed together with one accord, and they received the baptism in the Holy Spirit, preached the gospel, bore the testimony of Jesus, and always moved and acted as one Body (1:14; 2:1, 4, 14, 46-47).

It is difficult to find anyone among them who acted individualistically. Although it appears that Philip preached the gospel by himself in chapter eight when he was in Samaria, it was Peter and John who came to confirm his preaching (vv. 5, 14-17). The Holy Spirit, the power upon the Body, did not come upon those believers through Philip's preaching. It was when Peter and John came and laid hands on the Samaritan believers that the Holy Spirit on the Body was transmitted to them. This proves that even Philip's preaching...was related to the move of the Body. Therefore, chapter after chapter in the Acts records the move and activity of the Body, not of individual believers.

The activities recorded in Acts were not only of the Body but also for the Body, that is, for the building up of the church....The activities in this book are absolutely different from the movement of today's Christianity. Many in today's Christianity act in a way that is not of the Body or for the Body. As we have seen, the Acts is a record of a group of people who act and work all the time for the Body and through the Body. Therefore, in this book the churches are built up of out of the activities of those people. The Acts contains a beautiful picture of the one accord in the activities, work, and move of the believers. They always moved in the Body and for the Body. (*A General Sketch of the New Testament in the Light of Christ and the Church, Part 1: The Gospels and the Acts,* pp. 90-91)

The flowing of the divine life, which started on the day of Pentecost and has been flowing throughout all generations to this very day, is just one stream. Wherever it goes, wherever it flows, it is not many streams; it is only one. Read the book of Acts and there you will see that there is one stream, one current. This stream started from Jerusalem and flowed to Antioch, and from Antioch it turned to Asia and was flowing there. Then one day the Lord wanted the stream to strike forth into Europe. (*The Divine Stream,* p. 12)

Further Reading: A General Sketch of the New Testament in the Light of Christ and the Church, Part 1: The Gospels and the Acts, chs. 6-7; The Divine Stream

Enlightenment and inspiration: _____

_____

_____

Morning Nourishment

Acts **But you shall receive power when the Holy Spirit**
1:8 **comes upon you, and you shall be My witnesses both**
     in Jerusalem and in all Judea and Samaria and unto
     the uttermost part of the earth.
2:32 **This Jesus God has raised up, of which we all are**
     witnesses.

The central meaning of the flow in the Acts is that there is a
group of people who know the meaning of resurrection and ascension. They live not by themselves but by Christ as their life, and
they act not according to certain ways or methods but by the
living Christ as their strength, power, method, and way. Moreover,
they realize that they are the Body, and they always act in the
Body and for the Body in the one divine stream. May we all be
clear to such an extent that we not only know the resurrection
and ascension, but we live in resurrection and act in ascension,
not by ourselves but in the Body, for the Body, and in one flow. This
is the real meaning of the book of Acts. (*A General Sketch of the
New Testament in the Light of Christ and the Church, Part 1: The
Gospels and the Acts,* pp. 92-93)

Today's Reading

Acts 23:11 says, "...In the night following, the Lord stood by
him and said, Take courage, for as you have solemnly testified to
the things concerning Me in Jerusalem, so also you must testify in
Rome." The Lord was living all the time in Paul essentially (Gal.
2:20). Now, to strengthen and encourage him, the Lord stood by
him economically. This showed the Lord's faithfulness and good
care for His servant....The Lord admitted that the apostle had
borne a solemn testimony concerning Him in Jerusalem. Testimony differs from mere teaching. To testify requires experiences
of seeing, participation, and enjoyment.

What the ascended Christ wanted to use to carry out His heav-
enly ministry for the propagating of Himself so that the kingdom of
God might be established for the building up of the churches for
His fullness was not a group of preachers trained by man's

teaching to do a preaching work, but a body of His witnesses, martyrs, who bore a living testimony of the incarnated, crucified, resurrected, and ascended Christ. Witnesses bear a living testimony of the resurrected and ascended Christ in life. They differ from preachers who merely preach doctrines in letters. In His incarnation, Christ carried out His ministry on earth, as recorded in the Gospels, by Himself to sow Himself as the seed of the kingdom of God only in the Jewish land. In His ascension He carries out His ministry in the heavens, as recorded in Acts, through witnesses in His resurrection life and with His ascension power and authority to spread Himself as the development of the kingdom of God from Jerusalem unto the remotest part of the earth, as the consummation of His ministry in the New Testament. All the apostles and disciples in Acts were such witnesses of Christ.

In Acts 26:16 Paul testified that the Lord had appointed him a minister and a witness. A minister is for the ministry; a witness is for the testimony. Ministry is mainly related to work, to what the minister does; testimony is related to the person, to what the witness is.

Satan could instigate the Jewish religionists and utilize the Gentile politicians to bind the apostles and their evangelical ministry, but he could not bind Christ's living witnesses and their living testimonies. The more the Jewish religionists and Gentile politicians bound the apostles and their evangelical ministry, the stronger and brighter these martyrs, these witnesses, of Christ and their living testimonies became. The Lord...indicated that He would not presently rescue [Paul] from his bonds, but that He would leave him in bonds and bring him to Rome so that he might testify concerning Him as he had done in Jerusalem [23:11]…. Assured by this clear word from the mouth of the Lord, Paul knew that he would go to Rome and there bear the testimony of the Lord Jesus. (*Life-study of Acts,* pp. 542-543)

Further Reading: A General Sketch of the New Testament in the Light of Christ and the Church, Part 1: The Gospels and the Acts, ch. 8; *Life-study of Acts,* msgs. 62-63

Enlightenment and inspiration: _____

_____

_____

_____

Morning Nourishment

Acts   ...Of the men who accompanied us all the time in
1:21-22 which the Lord Jesus went in and went out among
us, beginning from the baptism of John until the day
on which He was taken up from us, one of these
should become a witness of His resurrection with us.
4:33 And with great power the apostles gave testimony of
the resurrection of the Lord Jesus, and great grace
was upon them all.

Acts 27:13-26 describes the storm and Paul's prediction of
safety....[Verses 20 and 21 say], "From then on all hope that we
might be saved was being abandoned....Paul then stood in their
midst and said, O men, you should have listened to me and not set
sail from Crete and gained this damage and loss." Although Paul
was a prisoner in bonds, his behavior displayed much ascendancy
with dignity. Luke's narration, as an account of the Lord's move
on earth, does not stress doctrine but the testimony of the Lord's
witnesses (1:8). Hence, in his narration there are no details of doctrines but of the events that occurred to His witnesses, in order to
portray their testimonies in their lives. It is especially so with
Paul's voyage in the last two chapters. Here Paul was a witness of
the Lord. Therefore, we should not read Luke's account merely as
a story of a storm at sea. Rather, we need to see in this story the
description of the life of one of Christ's living witnesses. (*Life-
study of Acts,* pp. 610-611)

Today's Reading

Speaking of Judas, Peter...[says] in Acts 1:17, "For he was
numbered among us and was allotted his portion of this ministry."
"This ministry," mentioned also in verse 25, is the ministry to bear
the testimony of Jesus (v. 8). Though the apostles were twelve in
number, their ministry was uniquely one—this ministry, a corporate ministry in the principle of the Body of Christ. All the apostles carried out the same ministry to bear the testimony not of
any religion, doctrine, or practice, but uniquely of the incarnated,
resurrected, and ascended Jesus Christ, the Lord of all.

Peter went on to say, "It is necessary therefore that of the men who accompanied us all the time in which the Lord Jesus went in and went out among us, beginning from the baptism of John until the day on which He was taken up from us, one of these should become a witness of His resurrection with us" (vv. 21-22). The Lord's resurrection is the focus of the apostles' testimony. It refers back to His incarnation, humanity, human living on earth, and God-ordained death (2:23), and points forward to His ascension, ministry and administration in heaven, and coming back. Thus the apostles' testimony of Jesus Christ, the Lord of all, is all-inclusive, as depicted in the whole book of Acts. They preached and ministered the all-inclusive Christ as revealed in the entire Scripture.

Acts 2:24 says that it was not possible for the Lord to be held by death. The Lord is both God and resurrection (John 1:1; 11:25), possessing the indestructible life (Heb. 7:16). Because He is such an ever-living One, death is not able to hold Him. He delivered Himself to death, but death had no way to detain Him; rather, death was defeated by Him, and He rose up from it.

In Acts 2:32 Peter gives a concluding word concerning Christ's resurrection: "This Jesus God has raised up, of which we all are witnesses." The Greek word for "which" here may also be rendered "whom." The apostles were witnesses of the resurrected Christ, not in word only, but also by their life and action. Especially they bore witness of His resurrection (4:33), which is the crucial focus in carrying out God's New Testament economy.

Acts 4:33 says, "And with great power the apostles gave testimony of the resurrection of the Lord Jesus, and great grace was upon them all."...Actually, grace is God Himself enjoyed by man. Grace is the resurrected Christ becoming the life-giving Spirit (1 Cor. 15:45) to bring the processed God in resurrection into us to be our life and life supply so that we may live in resurrection. Therefore, grace is the Triune God becoming life and everything to us. (*Life-study of Acts,* pp. 40, 78-79, 135-136)

Further Reading: Life-study of Acts, msgs. 5, 10, 17, 70

Enlightenment and inspiration: _____

_____

_____

_____

Morning Nourishment

Acts That God has fully fulfilled this *promise* to us their
13:33 children in raising up Jesus, as it is also written in
the second Psalm, "You are My Son; this day have I
begotten You."
Rom. Knowing that Christ, having been raised from the
6:9 dead, dies no more; death lords it over Him no more.

[In Acts 3:13 Peter says, "The God of Abraham and Isaac and
Jacob, the God of our fathers, has glorified His Servant Jesus,
whom you delivered up and denied in the presence of Pilate, when
he had decided to release Him."] Why...did Peter speak of God as
the God of Abraham, Isaac, and Jacob? Why did he not speak
simply of God? This title refers to the Triune God, Jehovah, the
great I AM (Exo. 3:14-15). According to the Lord's word in
Matthew 22, this divine title implies resurrection: "Concerning
the resurrection of the dead, have you not read that which was
spoken to you by God, saying, 'I am the God of Abraham and the
God of Isaac and the God of Jacob'? He is not the God of the dead,
but of the living" (vv. 31-32). Peter referred to God as the God of
Abraham, Isaac, and Jacob because this indicates that He is the
God of resurrection.

Peter told the people that the God of Abraham, Isaac, and
Jacob "glorified His Servant Jesus." God glorified the Lord Jesus
through His resurrection and in His ascension (Luke 24:26; Heb.
2:9; Eph. 1:20-22; Phil. 2:9-11). (*Life-study of Acts,* pp. 101-102)

Today's Reading

Resurrection was a birth to the man Jesus. He was begotten by
God in His resurrection to be the firstborn Son of God among many
brothers (Rom. 8:29). He was the only begotten Son of God from
eternity (John 1:18; 3:16). After incarnation, through resurrection,
He was begotten by God in His humanity to be God's firstborn Son.

If it were not for Paul, I do not think that we would be able to
see that Psalm 2 speaks of the resurrection of Christ. Paul was
able to see the Lord's resurrection in the word, "You are My Son; /
Today I have begotten You" [v. 7]. Paul applied the word "today" to

the day of the Lord's resurrection. This means that Christ's resurrection was His birth as the firstborn Son of God. Jesus, the Son of Man, was born to be the Son of God through being raised up from the dead. Therefore, God's raising up of Jesus from the dead was His begetting of Him to be His firstborn Son. We need to realize that the Lord's resurrection was His birth. This is a crucial matter. (*Life-study of Acts,* p. 318)

It was after the Lord's resurrection from the dead that God pronounced with joy, "You are My Son; / Today I have begotten You." Through the Lord's resurrection God secured the man He wants.

What is the meaning of resurrection? It means that a man has broken through all barriers, even the greatest barrier of all—death. All barriers were destroyed through the Lord Jesus in His resurrection. The New Testament speaks a few times of the raising of the dead....[However], only the Lord's resurrection was a total destruction of death. When He resurrected, He faced death no longer. The Bible shows us that only the Lord is resurrection....Man's biggest limitations are time and space, but these two things cannot limit the Lord. Resurrection means that all limitations have been broken. Hallelujah, our Lord Jesus is no longer bound by anything today! As long as we live in the Holy Spirit, we can touch the Lord. The Lord is in our midst, and all barriers are broken.

Death is the greatest limitation, but resurrection has conquered death. Therefore, resurrection is the greatest power of all. ...Even now we are only touching the hem of the resurrected Lord's garment; we are still far off. If we can touch a little more, we will transcend death and everything else. This is the greatest power of all. Once we touch the power of resurrection, it will be easy to spread the gospel of the kingdom to all of China. Resurrection power is the greatest of all powers. (*The Collected Works of Watchman Nee,* vol. 59, pp. 82-84)

Further Reading: Life-study of Acts, msgs. 13, 37; *The Conclusion of the New Testament,* msg. 30*

Enlightenment and inspiration: _____

_____

_____

_____

Morning Nourishment

Eph.   **And what is the surpassing greatness of His power**
1:19-20 **toward us who believe, according to the operation of**
        the might of His strength, which He caused to operate
        in Christ in raising Him from the dead...
Matt.   **...If two of you are in harmony on earth concerning**
18:19   **any matter for which they ask, it will be done for**
        them from My Father who is in the heavens.

The power of the Holy Spirit is the power of resurrection. This means that the Lord installed the power of resurrection and even resurrection itself into the Holy Spirit when He sent this Spirit to us. As soon as a man touches the Holy Spirit, he touches resurrection. Once a man is in the Spirit, he touches the Lord of resurrection. The Holy Spirit testifies to the resurrection of the Lord. While the Lord was on the earth, some leaned on His bosom. Others kissed Him, pressed upon Him, or received from His hands....However, this kind of touch cannot compare with our touch today. Today we are not bound by time and space. The resurrected Lord is now in the Holy Spirit. (*The Collected Works of Watchman Nee,* vol. 59, pp. 84-85)

Today's Reading

What is the church? The church is where the Lord is the Head and we are the Body. What is the relationship between the church and resurrection, and what is the relationship between the church and the Holy Spirit?...The church is the place where God demonstrates the operation of the might of His strength, according to the power which He caused to operate in Christ [Eph. 1:19-20]. We have to pay attention to the words *according to* [in verse 19]. They mean that God is causing the same degree of might and strength that operated in Christ to now operate in the church.... The church can now experience the same might and strength that the Lord experienced. The church is the same as the resurrected Lord not only in nature but also in power. If this were not so, everything about the church would be vanity. Just as God broke through all barriers in the Lord, He is breaking through all barriers in the church. Therefore, the church should be the same as the resurrected Lord. It should be as powerful, as free, and as unfettered by any limitation as the Lord is. Otherwise, it cannot be called the church. The might of God's strength not only operated in Christ, but it continually operates in the church as well. Today the church is the depository and storehouse of the power of resurrection. This is the church. Anything less than this will not do.

Today the church has received this power supply from the ascended and glorified Christ. Therefore, there is no problem that the church cannot solve and no temptation that the church cannot overcome because the power of the church is the resurrection power of Christ, the same power that subjected all things under His feet. It is no less than the very power that operated in Christ.

The church became the Body of Christ after the Lord's resurrection. The church is filled with all that He is; it is the very vessel which holds the resurrected Christ. This is the meaning of the church. The Lord Jesus has passed through everything and has inherited everything. Nevertheless, He is only the Head. The church is His Body; it bears His characteristics. The church is what Christ is in Himself.

Hallelujah, we do not need anything more than what we already have! All we need to see is the glory, the riches, and the vastness of what we already possess. The authority in heaven is glorious and great, but it is limited by the earth. As long as there are two persons on earth who know resurrection and who stand on resurrection ground today, they will shake the ends of the earth. Presently, we have only touched the hem of the garment of resurrection. The Lord has released His speaking on resurrection to us in these years. Praise Him! What He has given us is the topmost portion; there cannot be any further improvement because we have become the same as the Lord. (*The Collected Works of Watchman Nee,* vol. 59, pp. 86-87, 95)

Further Reading: The Collected Works of Watchman Nee, vol. 59, chs. 10-11

Enlightenment and inspiration: _____

_____

_____

_____

Hymns, #1280

1   We've become the Lord's dear brothers
Through His resurrection pow'r;
He desires many brothers
Sharing in His triumph hour!

> Jesus is our Elder Brother,
> First-born of God's sons is He;
> He came forth in resurrection,
> From religion He is free!
> As His church we come together;
> Oldness, form, and self deny;
> Just to meet with our Big Brother,
> Him alone to glorify!

2   In our Brother's resurrection
Resurrected we must meet,
Never in our natural standing—
This will make His joy complete!

3   Every day we must see Jesus
As we're eating of the Word;
Then we'll run to all the meetings
Burning, bubbling with the Lord!

4   In the meetings we are feasting
On the food unlimited.
Jesus always satisfies us,
Feeding us the living bread!

5   We would satisfy our Brother,
Even though our portion's small.
Every one must share his "new dish"
For the benefit of all!

6   Not for message or for speaker,
But to meet the Lord we're here;
Caring only for His presence,
We would see our Brother dear!

Composition for prophecy with main point and sub-points: _____

One Accord

Scripture Reading: Acts 1:14; 2:46; 4:24, 32; 5:12; 15:25; Rom. 15:5-6; 1 Cor. 1:10

Day 1   I. **In John 17 the Lord Jesus prayed for oneness, in Ephesians 2 He died to produce oneness, in John 20 He breathed the Spirit into us as the essence of oneness, and in Acts 1 we have the application of oneness.**

II. **The genuine one accord in the church is the practice of the oneness of the Body, which is the oneness of the Spirit (Eph. 4:3-6):**

A. The practice of the genuine one accord in the church is the application of the oneness; when oneness is practiced, it becomes one accord (Acts 1:14; 2:46).

B. The landmark that divides the Gospels and the Acts is the one accord among the one hundred twenty (Acts 1:14):

1. They had become one in the Body, and in that oneness they continued steadfastly with one accord in prayer (Eph. 4:3-6; Acts 1:14).

2. When the apostles and the believers practiced the church life, they practiced it in one accord (2:46; 4:24, 32; 5:12; 15:25).

C. If we practice the principle of the Body, we will have the one accord, for the one accord is the Body (Rom. 12:4-5; 15:5-6; 1 Cor. 12:12-13, 20, 27; 1:10).

Day 2   D. One accord is the master key to every blessing in the New Testament (Eph. 1:3; Psa. 133):

1. In order to receive God's blessing we must practice the oneness by the one accord (v. 1).

2. The blessing of God can come only upon a situation of one accord, the practice of the oneness.

III. **One accord refers to the harmony in our inner being, in our mind and will (Acts 1:14):**

A. In Acts 1:14 the Greek word *homothumadon,* used for "one accord," is strong and all-inclusive:

 1. This word comes from *homo,* "same," and *thumos,* "mind, will, purpose (soul, heart)" and denotes a harmony of feeling in one's entire being.

 2. We should be in the same mind and the same will with the same purpose around and within our soul and heart; this means that our entire being is involved.

 3. For the one hundred twenty to be in one accord meant that their entire beings were one (v. 14).

Day 3

B. In Matthew 18:19 the Greek word *sumphoneo* is used to signify the one accord:

 1. This word means "to be in harmony, or accord" and refers to the harmonious sound of musical instruments or voices; the harmony of inward feeling among the believers is like a harmonious melody.

 2. When we have one accord, we become a pleasing melody to God.

IV. **The practice of the oneness—the one accord—is according to the apostles' teaching (Acts 2:42, 46):**

A. There was one accord among the believers, and those who were in one accord continued steadfastly in the apostles' teaching (v. 42).

B. The apostles taught the same thing to all the saints in all the places and in all the churches; today we also must teach the same thing in all the churches in every country throughout the earth (1 Cor. 4:17; 7:17; 11:16; 14:33b-34; Matt. 28:19-20).

C. The prohibition against sowing two kinds of seed in one's vineyard may typify the prohibition against teaching differently in the church (Deut. 22:9; 1 Tim. 1:3-4; 6:3; cf. Luke 8:11):

 1. The church is God's vineyard, and in this

vineyard only one kind of seed, one kind of teaching, should be sown (1 Cor. 3:9b; Acts 2:42).

2. If we teach differently, sowing more than one kind of seed, the "produce" in the church will be forfeited.

Day 4
&
Day 5

V. **In practicing the one accord, we need to be in one spirit with one soul (Phil. 1:27; 2:2, 5; 4:2):**

A. We should be attuned in the same mind and in the same opinion; this is to be one in our soul (1 Cor. 1:10; Phil. 1:27; 2:2, 5; 4:2).

B. To be in one accord is to be one in our whole being; this results in our being one in our outward speaking (Rom. 15:5-6):

1. To have one mind and one mouth means that we have only one Head—Christ; we should think with the mind of Christ and speak with the mouth of the Head (Col. 1:18a; Phil. 2:2, 5; 4:2).

2. Whenever we are in one accord, we speak with one mouth (Rom. 15:6).

3. *With one accord* and *with one mouth* mean that even though we are many and all are speaking, we all "speak the same thing" (1 Cor. 1:10).

4. The only way to be with one accord and one mouth is to allow Christ the room to be everything in our heart and in our mouth so that God may be glorified (Eph. 3:17a, 21).

VI. **In order to be in one accord we need to have one heart and one way (Jer. 32:39; Acts 1:14; 2:46; 4:24):**

A. The believers should have one heart—to love God, to seek God, to live God, and to be constituted with God so that we may be His expression—and one way—the Triune God Himself as the inner law of life with its divine capacity (Mark 12:30; 2 Cor. 13:14; Eph. 3:16-17; Jer. 31:33-34; John 14:6a).

B. Divisions result from having a heart for something other than Christ and taking a way other than Christ (1 Cor. 1:13a; 2:2; Col. 2:8; Acts 15:35-40).

Day 6 **VII. If we would have one accord, there should be only one "scale" in the church life (Deut. 25:13-16):**

A. To condemn a certain thing in others while justifying the same thing in ourselves indicates that we have different weights and measures, that is, different scales—one scale for measuring others and a different scale for measuring ourselves.

B. The practice of having different scales is the source of disaccord, but if we have only one scale, we will keep the oneness and one accord in the church (Eph. 4:1-3; Matt. 7:1-5).

VIII. For the Lord's up-to-date move, all the churches need to be in one accord; we should all voice the same thing, trumpet the same thing, teach the same thing, and be the same in practice (Josh. 1:16-18; 6:1-16; Acts 2:42; 4:24, 32; 1 Cor. 4:17; 7:17; 11:16; 14:33b-34; 1 Tim. 1:3-4; 6:3).

Morning Nourishment

Acts These all continued steadfastly with one accord in
1:14 prayer...
2:46 And day by day, continuing steadfastly with one
      accord in the temple and breaking bread from
      house to house...
4:24 And when they heard *this*, they lifted up *their* voice
      with one accord to God...

In the Body we need oneness; in the churches and among the churches, we need the one accord. The one accord is for our practice; the oneness is primarily for the actuality, for the fact. In John 17 the Lord Jesus prayed for such a fact, and on the day of Pentecost, by pouring out Himself as the consummated Spirit, He accomplished His prayer. That was the actuality of the oneness. After the accomplishment of the actuality of the oneness, there is the need for the practice of the oneness. When the oneness is practiced, it becomes the one accord. The one accord is the practice of the oneness. (*The Intrinsic Problem in the Lord's Recovery Today and Its Scriptural Remedy*, pp. 23-24)

Today's Reading

If we have only the oneness as an actuality, and do not have the present, practical one accord, the oneness that we have will be objective and abstract; it will not be real to us. If we would apply the oneness accomplished by the outpouring of the Spirit, we must practice the one accord. If among us there is no one accord, how could we say that there is oneness? If in a prayer meeting we each pray in our own way, without any accord among us, how could we say that we are practicing the oneness? As long as we have differences existing among us, the oneness is not applied. We must have the one accord to swallow up all the differences; then oneness will be present.

The practice of the proper one accord in the church is the application of the oneness. Although oneness and one accord seem to be synonymous, there is a difference between them. The Lord did not teach us concerning oneness. In John 17 He prayed for oneness, but in Matthew 18 He led us to practice the one accord. In Matthew 18:19 the Lord spoke of two praying together on earth in one accord. That was His leading, His training, and His directing us to pray in one accord. (*The Intrinsic Problem in the Lord's Recovery Today and Its Scriptural Remedy,* p. 24)

We must realize that the practices in the Lord's recovery are not matters for others to copy. You must have the life. To do anything you need the life. You have to see [that]... the landmark that divides the Gospels and the Acts is not the baptism in the Holy Spirit. The landmark is the one accord of the one hundred twenty. If you want to experience the baptism in the Spirit, you must have the one accord. If all the members of a local church have the one accord, the baptism in the Spirit will be there. (*Elders' Training, Book 7: One Accord for the Lord's Move,* p. 18)

The oneness that the Lord aspired for and prayed for in John 17 corresponds with the oneness of the Spirit in Ephesians 4:3-6. We must see that the church is the Body of Christ, which is a constitution, an entity constituted with the Triune God and His chosen and redeemed ones. In this Body there is the reality of oneness....The real oneness is the organic oneness of the Body. In a locality, this oneness is called *one accord.* Without the oneness of the Body, there is no possibility to have one accord in the church.

The one accord is first mentioned in Acts 1. The one hundred twenty had become one in the Body, and in that oneness they continued steadfastly with one accord in prayer (v. 14). (*The Governing and Controlling Vision in the Bible,* p. 29)

We must practice the principle of the Body; then we will have the one accord. Although we may not fight with one another, we still may not have the one accord. Because we have remained together, we have seen the Lord's blessing, but only in a limited way. Therefore, we need to have the one accord to practice the Body. (*Fellowship concerning the Urgent Need of the Vital Groups,* p. 88)

Further Reading: The Intrinsic Problem in the Lord's Recovery Today and Its Scriptural Remedy, chs. 1-2

Enlightenment and inspiration: _____

_____

_____

_____

Morning Nourishment

Eph. **Blessed be the God and Father of our Lord Jesus**
1:3 **Christ, who has blessed us with every spiritual**
blessing in the heavenlies in Christ.
1 Cor. **For even as the body is one and has many members,**
12:12 **yet all the members of the body, being many, are one**
body, so also is the Christ.

If you really want to practice the proper way to preach the gospel, you need the one accord. Without this key, no door can be opened. The one accord is the "master key to all the rooms," the master key to every blessing in the New Testament. This is why Paul told Euodias and Syntyche that they needed this one accord (Phil. 4:2). Paul knew that these sisters loved the Lord, but that they had lost the one accord.

What we need is to recover this one accord. If we mean business to go along with the Lord's present day move, we need this one accord. ...We need to have the same mind and the same will for the same purpose with the same soul and the same heart. Philippians tells us that this matter starts from our spirit (1:27), yet we must realize we are not persons of spirit only. We are persons also of the mind, will, purpose, soul, and heart. For us to be in the same one spirit with the same one soul, one mind, and one will is to have the one accord, which is the key to all the New Testament blessings and bequests. (*Elders' Training, Book 7: One Accord for the Lord's Move*, pp. 18-19)

Today's Reading

We must be in one accord to maintain the oneness Christ seeks. ...We should see the way for the church to receive grace and blessing....The blessing and grace of God can only come upon a situation of one accord. This situation is the practice of oneness. In the Old Testament, Psalm 133 says, "Behold, how good and how pleasant it is for brothers to dwell in unity!...For there Jehovah commanded the blessing: Life forever." God will only grace and bless the one accord, that is, the practice of oneness. (*The Oneness and the One Accord according to the Lord's Aspiration and the Body*

Life and Service according to His Pleasure, p. 18)

The one accord refers to the harmony in our inner being, in our mind and will. In Matthew 18:19 the Lord said, "If two of you are in harmony on earth concerning any matter for which they ask, it will be done for them from My Father who is in the heavens." *In harmony* here is as musical sounds are in harmony. We need this harmony as our one accord. (*Fellowship concerning the Urgent Need of the Vital Groups,* p. 103)

After breathing Himself into His disciples, He stayed with them for forty days to train them to experience His invisible presence. He then ascended to the heavens, leaving the disciples on this earth.…[The one hundred twenty] did nothing except to pray, and the key of their prayer was the one accord (Acts 1:14).

In Matthew 18:19 the Lord spoke concerning two or three being in harmony…in prayer. The word for "harmony"… is not as strong as the word "one accord." The word in Greek for one accord, *homothumadon,* is strong and all-inclusive. *Homo* means the same and *thumos* means mind, will, purpose (soul, heart).

In the book of Acts the one hundred twenty prayed together in one mind, in the same mind, in the same will with the same purpose around and within the soul and the heart. Whenever we pray, we surely should exercise our spirit, but we also should be in the same mind and the same will with the same purpose around and within our soul and heart. This means that our entire being is involved. After the Lord's ascension, the one hundred twenty became the kind of persons who were in one mind, in one will, with one purpose around their soul and heart. For them to be in one accord meant that their entire beings were one. No other book of the Bible uses the word for "one accord" as much as Acts. (*Elders' Training, Book 7: One Accord for the Lord's Move,* pp. 10-11)

Further Reading: The Oneness and the One Accord according to the Lord's Aspiration and the Body Life and Service according to His Pleasure, ch. 1; *Elders' Training, Book 7: One Accord for the Lord's Move,* chs. 1-2

Enlightenment and inspiration: _____

_____

_____

_____

Morning Nourishment

Matt. ...If two of you are in harmony on earth concerning any
18:19 matter for which they ask, it will be done for them...

Acts And they continued steadfastly in the teaching and
2:42 the fellowship of the apostles, in the breaking of bread
and the prayers.

1 Cor. ...Even as I teach everywhere in every church.
4:17

What is the one accord?...Apparently, oneness is a great thing, whereas one accord is a smaller matter. It is easy to define oneness: oneness is the Triune God mingled with all His believers, and this oneness is just the Body of Christ. However, it is difficult to define one accord.

In Matthew 18:19 the Greek word *sumphoneo* is used for one accord. It means "to be in harmony, or accord" and refers to the harmonious sound of musical instruments or voices. Eventually, the one accord, or the harmony of inward feeling among the believers, becomes like a melody, like music....When we have the one accord, in the eyes of God we become a melody to Him. We become a poem not merely in writing but in sound, in voice, in melody. Our one accord must be like a harmonious melody. Such a one accord is the nucleus of the oneness. In other words, oneness is like a nut, and the one accord is like the kernel of that nut. (*Fellowship concerning the Urgent Need of the Vital Groups*, p. 76)

Today's Reading

From Ephesians 4:4-6 we can see that our practice of oneness is based upon the attribute of the oneness of the church: one Spirit, one Lord, one God, one Body, one faith, one baptism, and one hope. By this we can see that oneness is the attribute of the church. Based upon this attribute of the oneness of the church, we can be in one accord and can practice the oneness. Moreover, the practice of this oneness is according to the apostles' teaching (1 Cor. 4:17b; 7:17b; 11:16; 14:34a). The apostles taught the same thing to all the saints in all the places and in all the churches. At the same time, the practice of this oneness is also according to the same speaking of the Spirit to the churches (Rev. 2:7, 11a, 17a, 29; 3:6, 13, 22). The seven epistles to the seven churches in Revelation 2 and 3 were words spoken to all the churches....Each epistle was written to all the churches. All the churches have the same Bible, and everyone is practicing oneness according to the same speaking. (*The Oneness and the One Accord according to the Lord's Aspiration and the Body Life and Service according to His Pleasure,* pp. 17-18)

We are not for the teachings which can be considered as winds, but we are for the oneness of the unique faith which is the very contents of God's New Testament economy. To have different teachings in the Lord's recovery is altogether not authentic. We have to keep the principle of one teaching, not my teaching nor your teaching but the teaching of the apostles. Our one teaching has to be the teaching which is our faith, the very contents of which are the New Testament Bible, the very constituents of God's New Testament economy. This is the teaching we should pass on, and this is the teaching all the churches should take and should remain in. By this way we surely can be one in one teaching. (*Elders' Training, Book 7: One Accord for the Lord's Move,* p. 43)

"You shall not sow your vineyard with two kinds of seed, lest the full produce...be forfeited to the sanctuary..." (Deut. 22:9).... If an Israelite sowed two kinds of seed in his vineyard, neither the produce of that seed nor the increase of the vineyard would be his. He was not allowed to keep them for himself....This means that his labor in sowing his vineyard with two kinds of seed would be in vain.

I believe that the prohibition against sowing two kinds of seed in one's vineyard typifies the prohibition against teaching different things in the church (1 Tim. 1:3). The church is God's vineyard, and in this vineyard we should sow only one kind of seed, one kind of teaching. If we teach different things, sowing more than one kind of seed, the "produce" in the church will be forfeited. (*Life-study of Deuteronomy,* p. 155)

Further Reading: Elders' Training, Book 9: The Eldership and the God-ordained Way (1), ch. 1; *Fellowship concerning the Urgent Need of the Vital Groups,* msgs. 9-10

Enlightenment and inspiration: _____

_____

_____

_____

Morning Nourishment

Phil. Only, conduct yourselves in a manner worthy of the
1:27 gospel of Christ, that...I may hear of the things concerning you, that you stand firm in one spirit, with one
soul striving together *along* with the faith of the gospel.
2:2 Make my joy full, that you think the same thing, having
the same love, joined in soul, thinking the one thing.
Rom. That with one accord you may with one mouth glorify
15:6 the God and Father of our Lord Jesus Christ.

The proper one accord in the church is the practice of the
genuine oneness of the Body (Matt. 18:19; Acts 1:14). In Matthew
18:19, before the Lord prayed for the oneness in John 17, He
trained His disciples to practice the one accord. Actually,...to be in
the one accord is to practice the oneness. A little more than forty
days after the Lord's prayer in John 17, the one hundred twenty
disciples practiced the Lord's direction in Matthew 18 by praying
together in one accord (Acts 1:14).

When we practice the one accord, we must learn to be in one
spirit and with one soul (Phil. 1:27). We may be bodily sitting
together in the same room, but if we are not one in our spirit, it is
certain that we will not be one in our soul. To practice the one accord,
we must learn to turn to our spirit and then to enter into our soul
with the spirit that we may be in the one accord. (*Elders' Training,
Book 10: The Eldership and the God-ordained Way (2),* pp. 53-54)

Today's Reading

To practice the one accord, we must be attuned in the same
mind and in the same opinion (1 Cor. 1:10). To be attuned in the
same mind is to practically be one in our soul. When the thoughts
in our mind are expressed in our speaking, they become our opinions. When the opinions remain in our mind, they are simply our
thoughts. When our differences in thinking are expressed as
opinions, that may cause a problem. (*Elders' Training, Book 10:
The Eldership and the God-ordained Way (2),* p. 54)

Romans 15:6 tells us that we should be "with one accord" and
"with one mouth." The word "accord" includes the mind, will,

and purpose in the soul and the heart. We need to have one mind and one mouth. This means that we only have one Head because only the head has a mouth and a mind. We all take the Lord Jesus as the Head. Only He is fully qualified to have the mind and to have the mouth. We do not have the right because we are members of the Body. We do not have the mouth or the mind so we have to think with the mind of Christ (Phil 2:2, 5; 4:2). Then we have to speak with the mouth of the Head. The mouth only has one head.

If we considered this matter, we would not speak so loosely or freely; we would not speak whatever we like. You may like to speak something which the Head does not like. You are not the mouth. In the whole universe there is only one new man, and the one new man only has one Head with one Body. The mouth is not on the Body but with the Head. We must learn not to speak things so easily. Your speaking interferes with or profanes the mouth of the Head. You do not have any mouth. What the church has as the mouth is the mouth of the Head.

What does it mean that we all have one mind and one mouth? This means "no longer I...but...Christ who lives in me" (Gal. 2:20a). It is no more I, but Christ the Head that lives in me. He has a mouth, He has a mind, and I take Him as my person, so I would never use my mouth any longer to speak anything....We need to practice the one mouth to be one in speaking. (*Elders' Training, Book 7: One Accord for the Lord's Move*, pp. 44-45)

We need to be of the same mind toward one another according to Christ Jesus so that with one accord we may glorify God in receiving the believers to live the church life (Rom. 15:5-7)....The only way to be with one accord and with one mouth is to allow Christ the room to be everything in our heart and in our mouth that God may be glorified. (*The Experience of God's Organic Salvation Equaling Reigning in Christ's Life*, p. 63)

Further Reading: Elders' Training, Book 10: The Eldership and the God-ordained Way (2), ch. 4; *Life-study of Philippians*, msgs. 2, 8; *Life-study of Romans*, msg. 29

Enlightenment and inspiration: _____

_____

_____

_____

Morning Nourishment

Jer. **And I will give them one heart and one way, to fear**
32:39 **Me all the days, for their own good and for *the good***
of their children after them.
Mark **"And you shall love the Lord your God from your**
12:30 **whole heart and from your whole soul and from**
your whole mind and from your whole strength."
John **Jesus said to him, I am the way...**
14:6

All of us need to be one with the Lord in the life pulse of His
new move. For the Lord's new move, all of the churches need to be
in one accord. In the past, we lost the one accord, but we must
endeavor to recover and keep it. We also must teach the same
thing in all the churches in every country throughout the earth.
There should be no different trumpeting or different voicing
among us. We should all voice the same thing, trumpet the same
thing, and teach the same thing. (*Elders' Training, Book 9: The
Eldership and the God-ordained Way (1)*, p. 16)

Today's Reading

Today the Lord wants to present a positive testimony for Christianity to see that Christians can certainly be one....By the Lord's
grace it is more than possible!...Without the Lord's mercy and grace,
all of us descendants of Adam are "little demons," and no one can be
one with anyone else. But on the day of Pentecost the Lord came in,
and those speakers of different dialects immediately became one
in the Lord....Every one of us can boast, "Hallelujah, today I am in
Christ. In Christ we all have the Lord and His grace, so we are all
one. We can be one; this is absolutely possible!" It is possible because
we are all in the Lord and have His grace. (*One Body, One Spirit,
and One New Man*, pp. 94-95)

According to Jeremiah 32:38, Israel would be Jehovah's people, and He would be their God. After making this promise, Jehovah said, "I will give them one heart and one way, to fear Me all
the days, for their own good and for the good of their children after
them" (v. 39). We, the chosen people of God, should all have one
heart and one way. We should have one heart to love God, to seek

God, to live God, and to be constituted with God. This means that we love to be the expression of God. The one way is just the Triune God. The Lord Jesus said, "I am the way" (John 14:6a).

Christians today are divided because they take many different ways other than Christ. The Catholic Church has the Catholic way, and the Orthodox Church has the Orthodox way. Each denomination and independent group has its own way. The Presbyterians have one way, and the Pentecostals have another way.

What should be our way in the Body of Christ? As the Body of Christ, we should take the way of the inner law, which is the Triune God with His divine capacity. We should all have one heart to love Him, and we should all take Him as our life and our way. This one heart and one way is the one accord (Acts 1:14). If we do not have one heart and one way, we cannot be in one accord.

For eternity in the New Jerusalem there will be only one way. John tells us, "He showed me a river of water of life, bright as crystal, proceeding out of the throne of God and of the Lamb in the middle of its street. And on this side and on that side of the river was the tree of life, producing twelve fruits, yielding its fruit each month" (Rev. 22:1-2a). In the middle of the street, the river of water of life flows, and in the river the tree of life grows. This indicates that the way, the life, and the life supply are all one. It also indicates what our way should be today. Our way in the Lord's recovery is life; it is the inner law of life; it is the very Triune God Himself.

In recent years there was a turmoil among us, and this turmoil brought in division. The reason for this turmoil was that certain ones wanted to take a way other than life, a way other than Christ, the Triune God, and the inner law. Divisions are always the result of taking a way other than Christ. If we keep ourselves to the one way, there will be no division. We praise the Lord that in His restoration He will give His people one heart to love Him and express Him and one way to enjoy Him. (*Life-study of Jeremiah,* pp. 188-190)

Further Reading: Life-study of Jeremiah, msg. 27; *Elders' Training, Book 7: One Accord for the Lord's Move,* ch. 8

Enlightenment and inspiration: _____

_____

_____

_____

Morning Nourishment

1 Cor.   ...If anyone seems to be contentious, we do not have
11:16   such a custom *of being so,* neither the churches of God.
Phil.   If there is therefore any encouragement in Christ, if
2:1-2   any consolation of love, if any fellowship of spirit, if any
          tenderheartedness and compassions, make my joy full,
          that you think the same thing, having the same love,
          joined in soul, thinking the one thing.

All of the churches should...be one in practice (1 Cor. 11:16; 14:33b-34). If the churches are not the same in practice, this will damage the one accord. If we train the full-timers in the God-ordained way, and they return to churches who practice differently, this could cause problems. We will be contradicting ourselves. I hope that all the trainees who return to their churches will be so useful because we are all practicing the same way.

In the early days of the church life, the churches were the same in practice. When Paul went to Jerusalem, however, he saw something different (Acts 21:20; see James 2:10 and footnote 1). Eventually, the Lord wiped out that different thing in Jerusalem. In the past we suffered much loss because of our different ways to practice the church life....In the Lord's recovery, there should only be one work in one move with one ministry for the building up of the one Body. (*Elders' Training, Book 9: The Eldership and the God-ordained Way (1),* pp. 16-17)

Today's Reading

Deuteronomy 25:13-16 covers the judgment concerning weights and measures. The children of Israel were not to have in their bag differing weights, one heavy and one light, nor were they to have in their house differing measures, one heavy and one light (vv. 13-14). For everyone who did these things, everyone who did unrighteousness, was an abomination to Jehovah their God (v. 16). To have differing weights and measures is a lie, and all lies come from the enemy, Satan.

Those who have differing weights and measures actually have differing scales. In the church life today, we may have differing scales—one scale for measuring others and a different scale for measuring ourselves. Having differing scales, we may condemn a certain thing in others but justify the same thing in ourselves. Certain saints may use one scale to weigh the actions of the elders and the co-workers but a different scale in weighing their own actions....[Thus], they find fault with the elders and co-workers but vindicate themselves.

In the house of God, the church, there should be only one scale. This means that the same scale should be used to weigh everyone. If we have only one scale, we will be fair, righteous, and just. ...Because God is fair, righteous, and just, He measures everyone according to the same scale.

[Nevertheless], we all have failed in this matter. Not one of us is an exception. Using the language of accounting, we may say that it is easy for us to "debit" others and "credit" ourselves....For instance, a sister may weigh the elders in one scale, giving them a debit, and weigh herself in a differing scale, giving herself a credit. If she would give the elders more credit and give herself more debit, she would have a much more positive view of the elders and of the church in her locality. However, if she persists in using different scales, none of the elders will be satisfactory in her eyes.

Some saints who have the practice of using differing scales may move from one locality to another, hoping to find a more satisfactory church with more satisfactory elders. But because these saints have differing scales, no matter where they may go, they do not find the church and the elders to be satisfactory.

I emphasize the practice of having differing scales because this practice is a sickness, a disease, in the church life. This is the source of disaccord. Instead of keeping the oneness and the one accord, we have disaccord. May we all receive mercy from the Lord to no longer have differing scales but, like our God, to have the same scale for everyone. (*Life-study of Deuteronomy,* pp. 134-136)

Further Reading: Elders' Training, Book 7: One Accord for the Lord's Move, chs. 3-5

Enlightenment and inspiration: _____
_____
_____
_____

Hymns, #258

1   "With one accord" within an upper room
    The faithful followers of Jesus met:
    One was the hope of every waiting soul,
    And on one object great each heart was set.

2   "With one accord," until the mighty gift
    Of pentecostal power was outpoured;
    Then forth as witnesses possessed of God,
    To preach the resurrection of the Lord!

3   "With one accord" within the house of God
    A hallelujah song is daily raised,
    As with the voice of one, from vocal hearts
    Christ Jesus' name is glorified and praised.

4   Pour down Thy Spirit once again, dear Lord;
    Our cry goes up to Thee for "latter rain";
    Unite Thy people as the "heart of one,"
    And pentecostal days shall come again!

Composition for prophecy with main point and sub-points: _____

_____
_____
_____
_____
_____
_____
_____
_____
_____
_____
_____
_____
_____
_____
_____
_____
_____
_____
_____
_____
_____
_____
_____
_____
_____
_____
_____
_____
_____
_____
_____
_____
_____
_____
_____
_____
_____

The Holy Spirit in Acts—
the Essential Spirit of Resurrection Life and
the Economical Spirit of Ascension Power,
the Baptism in the Holy Spirit,
and
the Inward and Outward Filling of the Spirit

Scripture Reading: Luke 24:49; John 20:22; Acts 1:5, 8; 2:4, 33; 4:8; 6:3; 13:52; 1 Cor. 12:13

Day 1 I. **The Scriptures reveal that there are two aspects of the work of the Holy Spirit: the inward aspect for life—the essential Spirit— and the outward aspect for power and authority—the economical Spirit (John 14:17; 20:22; Luke 24:49; Acts 1:5, 8):**

A. *Essential* refers to the existence, to the being, and to the life for existence; *economical* refers to work, function, and power.

B. As a man, Christ Himself experienced these two aspects of the Holy Spirit:

1. He was born of the Holy Spirit essentially for His being and living, and He was anointed with the Holy Spirit economically for His ministry and move (Luke 1:35; Matt. 1:18, 20; 3:16; Luke 4:18).

2. The essential Spirit was within Him, and the economical Spirit was upon Him (Matt. 1:18, 20; Luke 4:18).

Day 2 C. In principle, both aspects of the Spirit are the same with us as they were with the Lord Jesus; every believer in Christ should experience both aspects of the Spirit (24:49; John 14:17; 20:22):

1. Inwardly we need to drink of the Holy Spirit for life, and outwardly we need to be clothed with the Holy Spirit for power and authority (1 Cor. 12:13; Luke 24:49; Acts 1:5, 8).

2. Inwardly we need the breath of the Holy Spirit breathed into us for life, and outwardly

we need the wind of the Holy Spirit blowing
upon us for power (John 20:22; Acts 2:2, 4):

   a. The inward aspect is the Holy Spirit as life
      within us (Rom. 8:2, 11).

   b. The outward aspect is the Holy Spirit as
      power upon us (Acts 1:8).

   c. As believers, we need the Spirit of life
      inwardly and the Spirit of power out-
      wardly; we must be filled inwardly with
      the Spirit as life and clothed outwardly
      with the Holy Spirit as power (Eph. 5:18;
      Luke 24:49).

Day 3   3. To experience the Spirit as our life for our
      spiritual being and existence is essential; to
      experience the Spirit as power for our spiri-
      tual work and function is economical (Rom.
      8:11; Luke 24:49; Acts 1:5, 8):

   a. On the day of resurrection, the Lord
      breathed the Spirit of life into the disci-
      ples; this is essential (John 20:22).

   b. On the day of Pentecost, the Lord poured
      out the Spirit of power upon the disciples;
      this is economical (Acts 2:1-4).

   4. Regarding the Spirit of life, we need to
      breathe Him in as the breath; regarding the
      Spirit of power, we need to put Him on as
      the uniform, typified by the mantle of Elijah
      (John 20:22; Luke 24:49; 2 Kings 2:9, 13-15):

   a. The former, like the water of life, requires
      our drinking; the latter, like the water of
      baptism, requires our being immersed
      (John 7:37-39; Acts 1:5).

   b. The essential indwelling of the Spirit of life
      and the economical outpouring of the
      Spirit of power are the two aspects of
      the one Spirit for our experience (1 Cor.
      12:13; *Hymns,* #278).

Day 4 **II. The baptism in the Holy Spirit is the out-
      pouring of the consummated Triune God as**

the all-inclusive compound Spirit by the Head
upon His Body (Luke 24:49; Acts 1:5, 8; 2:1-4;
10:44-47; 11:15-17; 1 Cor. 12:13):

A. Through the baptism in the Holy Spirit, the
believers were put together to form the Body of
Christ, joined to Him as the Head (v. 13).

B. The real meaning of the baptism in the Holy
Spirit is that we are immersed in the Triune God
and that we put on the Triune God as our uniform
(Luke 24:49).

C. The baptism in the Holy Spirit was accomplished
in two sections:

   1. All the Jewish believers were baptized in the
   Holy Spirit on the day of Pentecost (Acts 2:1-4).

   2. All the Gentile believers were baptized in the
   Holy Spirit in the house of Cornelius (10:44-47;
   11:15-17).

   3. In these two sections all genuine believers in
   Christ were baptized in the Holy Spirit into
   the one Body of Christ once for all universally
   (1 Cor. 12:13).

Day 5   D. There are five historical cases of the outpouring of
the Spirit recorded in Acts, only two of which are
called the baptism in the Holy Spirit:

   1. In these two cases Christ as the Head baptized the Jewish and Gentile parts of His Body
   in the Holy Spirit once for all; by so doing, He
   fully accomplished the baptism in the Holy
   Spirit upon His Body (Acts 1:5; 11:15-17).

   2. In the other cases the baptism in the Holy
   Spirit that had already been accomplished
   upon the Body by the Head was transmitted
   to the new members of the Body through
   identification with the Body; these three
   cases were experiences of the one baptism in
   the Holy Spirit, which the Body of Christ had
   already received (8:15-17; 9:17; 19:1-7).

E. The baptism in the Holy Spirit is uniquely one
and has been accomplished upon the Body once

for all; the experiences of the baptism in the Holy
Spirit are numerous and may be shared continually by the members of the Body who have a
proper understanding and realization (4:8; 13:9):

Day 6
1. We need to realize that the Lord has
   ascended and that He is the Lord and the
   Head over all things to the church (Luke
   24:50-51; Acts 1:9-11; 2:33-34; Eph. 1:19-23).
2. The baptism of the Body in the Holy Spirit is
   an accomplished fact and now exists upon
   the Body, ready for us to apply; this fact is a
   bequest given to us through the New Testament as a will (Luke 22:20; Heb. 8:8, 13).
3. We need to be right with the Body, stand in
   the Body, believe the will, and take the baptism in the Holy Spirit by faith (1 Cor. 12:13;
   Heb. 11:1, 6).

III. **As believers in Christ, we should experience
both the inward and the outward filling of the
Spirit (Eph. 5:18; Acts 2:4; 4:8; 6:3; 13:9, 52):**
   A. To be filled with the Spirit inwardly is to experi-
      ence the essential Spirit as life (Eph. 5:18; Acts
      6:3; 13:52).
   B. To be filled with the Spirit outwardly is to experi-
      ence the baptism in the Spirit for power and
      authority (1:5, 8; 2:4; 4:8; 13:9).
   C. When we are filled with the Spirit both inwardly
      and outwardly, we are completely mingled with
      the Triune God, who fills us, occupies us, and
      covers us; inwardly and outwardly, everywhere
      and in everything, there is the Spirit as the con-
      summation of the processed Triune God (1 Cor.
      12:13).

Morning Nourishment

Matt. Now the origin of Jesus Christ was in this way: His
1:18 mother, Mary, after she had been engaged to Joseph,
before they came together, was found to be with child
of the Holy Spirit.

20 ...That which has been begotten in her [Mary] is of
the Holy Spirit.

Luke "The Spirit of the Lord is upon Me, because He has
4:18 anointed Me...; He has sent Me..."

The very Spirit of life (Rom. 8:2) as the breath breathed into us is absolutely for life. We have the Triune God in His humanity with His human living, His all-inclusive death, and His excellent resurrection within us as our life. This is satisfying to the uttermost, but we still need the equipment, the power, the authority, the heavenly uniform. After ten days of prayer, the exalted, pneumatic Christ was poured out upon the disciples. He was breathed into them on the evening of the day of the resurrection as their life essentially, and He was poured out upon them on the day of Pentecost as their authority, as their mantle, as their clothing, as their heavenly uniform economically. Our friends, colleagues, neighbors, and family may not realize that we are wearing the exalted, pneumatic Christ as our uniform, but every demon and evil spirit knows this. They know that we are authorized and that we are part of the ascended Christ. (*God's New Testament Economy,* p. 95)

Today's Reading

"Essential" refers to the existence, to the being, and to the life for existence; "economical" refers to economy, work, and function. When we say the essential Trinity, we mean the divine Trinity in His existence, referring to His being. When we say the economical Trinity, we mean the divine Trinity in His economy, referring to His move, work, and function. To experience the Triune God as our life for our spiritual being, spiritual existence, is essential. To experience the Triune God as power for our spiritual work and spiritual function, is economical. To feed on the Lord as food, to drink Him as water, and to breathe Him as air is essential because it is related to the inner life for our spiritual existence. To put on the Lord as our clothing, to be clothed with the outpoured Spirit as power from on high, is economical because it is related to the outward move and work. On the day of resurrection, the Lord breathed the Spirit of life into the disciples. That is essential. On the day of Pentecost, the Lord poured out the Spirit of power upon the disciples. This is economical. On the one hand, they received the Spirit of life into their being essentially, and on the other hand, they received the Spirit of power upon them economically. Eventually, they became persons of the all-inclusive Spirit as the ultimate consummation of the processed Triune God. (*God's New Testament Economy,* pp. 95-96)

[The Spirit came] to Jesus Christ as both the divine essence and the divine power. First, the Spirit came as the divine essence for the conceiving and birth of Jesus (Luke 1:35; Matt. 1:18, 20). This was the coming of the Spirit essentially for Christ's existence and being as the God-man. The Lord Jesus was conceived of the divine essence, and this essence constituted His being.

In the conceiving of the God-man, the Holy Spirit came into humanity. The God-man was conceived of the Holy Spirit not only with the divine nature but also with the divine essence.... [Thus], He has the divine essence, the essence of God.

The Holy Spirit also came to Jesus Christ as the divine power for the anointing of Christ (Matt. 3:16). This was economical and was for Christ's ministry and work, whereas the coming of the Spirit as the divine essence was essential and was for the Lord's being and living. When He came forth at the age of thirty to minister and work for God, He needed the Spirit as His power economically.

Matthew 3:16 says, "He saw the Spirit of God descending like a dove and coming upon Him." Before the Spirit of God descended and came upon the Lord Jesus, He had already been born of the Spirit, which proved that He had the Spirit within Him. That was for His birth. Now, for His ministry, the Spirit of God descended upon Him. (*The Conclusion of the New Testament,* pp. 903-904)

Further Reading: Life-study of Mark, msgs. 67-68

Enlightenment and inspiration: _____

_____

_____

_____

Morning Nourishment

John   And when He had said this, He breathed into *them*
20:22   and said to them, Receive the Holy Spirit.
Luke   And behold, I send forth the promise of My Father
24:49   upon you; but as for you, stay in the city until you put
          on power from on high.
1 Cor.   For also in one Spirit we were all baptized into one
12:13   Body...and were all given to drink one Spirit.

We have seen that the Spirit came to Jesus Christ in two ways. First, the Spirit came essentially for the Lord's being, His existence. Second, the Spirit came to Him economically for His work, His ministry. In principle, both aspects of the Holy Spirit are the same with us....With Him there was the essential aspect for His being and the economical aspect for His ministry. With us there is also the essential aspect of the Spirit for our spiritual existence as regenerated believers, and there is the outward aspect of the Spirit for our Christian work. Therefore, we need to see how the Spirit comes to the New Testament believers both essentially and economically. (*The Conclusion of the New Testament,* p. 909)

Today's Reading

In Acts 2:2, the Holy Spirit is likened to "a rushing violent wind." The rushing violent wind is for power. It does have something to do with the breath, for it is the wind that brings the fresh air to breathe. But the main significance of the wind is power. The breath is for life, and the wind is for power.

John, in his Gospel, used drinking water and breath as two symbols of the Holy Spirit. That is the inward aspect for life, for John's Gospel is mainly concerned with life. However, Luke used two other symbols: clothing and the mighty wind. The writings of Luke (his Gospel and Acts) do not emphasize the matter of life, but the preaching of the gospel (Luke 24:47; Acts 1:8). In preaching the gospel, authority and power are needed. So clothing represents authority, and the rushing violent wind the power. If a policeman attempts to exercise his authority without wearing the proper uniform, no one will respect his authority; but when wearing the proper uniform, everyone honors his authority to act in the capacity of a law-enforcer. Even so, we must be clothed with the Holy Spirit that we may have divine authority and power for God's work.

Both aspects of the work of the Holy Spirit are necessary to us. Inwardly we need to drink of the Holy Spirit for life, and outwardly we need to be clothed with the Holy Spirit for authority. Inwardly we need the breath of the Holy Spirit breathed into us for life, and outwardly we need the wind of the Holy Spirit blowing upon us for power....The inward aspect of life is for our inward experience, and the outward aspect of power is for our outward experience. The inward aspect is "in" us (John 14:17; 4:14; 7:38), while the outward aspect is "upon" or "on" us (Luke 24:49; Acts 1:8; 2:3; 8:16; 10:44; 19:6). (*The Baptism in the Holy Spirit,* pp. 4-5)

As Christians we need both the Holy Spirit as the Spirit of life inwardly and the Holy Spirit as the Spirit of power outwardly....If we would be living, functioning members of the Body of Christ, we must be filled inwardly with the Holy Spirit as life, and we must be clothed outwardly with the Holy Spirit as power. Then we will be strong in life and equipped with power for our function in the Body. If, when we come together as believers meeting before the Lord, there is a lack of function in our midst, it is due to [a lack in] these two matters.

When I was called by the Lord to serve Him, I soon realized that I lacked something both inwardly and outwardly....I went to the Lord and consecrated myself to Him over and over again. I waited on the Lord, willing to be dealt with. I learned how to exercise my spirit to cooperate with Him, and I learned how to deny myself....Praise the Lord, after a time I knew that I had been both filled with the Holy Spirit inwardly and clothed with the Holy Spirit outwardly. Oh, from that time everything was different. My ministry was changed, and there was a real release. (*The Four Major Steps of Christ,* pp. 52-54)

Further Reading: The Conclusion of the New Testament, msgs. 84-85; *The Four Major Steps of Christ,* ch. 4

Enlightenment and inspiration: _____

_____

_____

_____

Morning Nourishment

John As...I live because of the Father, so he who eats Me,
6:57 he also shall live because of Me.
Acts For John baptized with water, but you shall be bap-
1:5 tized in the Holy Spirit not many days from now.
8 But you shall receive power when the Holy Spirit
comes upon you, and you shall be My witnesses...

According to John 20, in the evening of His resurrection day, the Lord appeared to His disciples, breathed on them, and said to them, "Receive the Holy Spirit" (v. 22). In this verse the Holy Spirit is likened to breath. Breath is something inward, something related to the life within us. In John 20:22, therefore, the disciples received the Holy Spirit as breath for life.

Forty days after His resurrection, the Lord commanded the disciples to remain in Jerusalem for the Holy Spirit to descend upon them [Acts 1:4-5, 8]. That descending of the Spirit upon the disciples was for power, not for life. In John 20 we have the Spirit inwardly for life; in Acts 1 we have the Spirit outwardly for power, for baptism. When a person is baptized, he does not drink the water; instead, he is immersed in the water. In a similar way, the baptism in the Holy Spirit is a matter of the Spirit coming upon us outwardly so that we may have power. (*Life-study of Mark*, p. 566)

Today's Reading

The disciples...received the Holy Spirit both essentially and economically. They received the Spirit essentially in John 20:22. The receiving of the essential Spirit was for their spiritual existence, their spiritual being. When the disciples received the Holy Spirit in John 20, they received the divine essence. After receiving the Spirit in this aspect for their spiritual existence, it was still necessary for them to receive the Spirit economically so that they could carry out God's economy as the continuation of the Lord Jesus. The disciples had to carry out God's economy in the same way the Lord Jesus carried it out....The disciples had to carry out God's economy by the economical Spirit. Therefore, after receiving the Spirit essentially, the disciples needed to receive the Spirit economically.

Before John 20, that is, before the Lord's death and resurrection, the disciples had not been made alive in their spiritual being for their spiritual existence. Instead, they had a fallen, natural, fleshly being. Even after the Lord had revealed to them His death and resurrection the third time (Mark 10:32-34), the disciples were still disputing concerning who was greater (Mark 10:35-45). …But after Christ's death and resurrection, the disciples received the essential Spirit as the source of their spiritual being.

The disciples had the essential Spirit for their spiritual being, but they still needed the Holy Spirit to descend upon them economically. This took place on the day of Pentecost. (*Life-study of Mark*, pp. 567-568)

In Acts 1:8 the Lord went on to say, "But you shall receive power when the Holy Spirit comes upon you, and you shall be My witnesses both in Jerusalem and in all Judea and Samaria and unto the uttermost part of the earth." To receive power is to be baptized in the Holy Spirit (v. 5) for the fulfillment of the promise of the Father (v. 4).

To have the Holy Spirit upon us is different from having the Holy Spirit in us (John 14:17). The Holy Spirit was breathed into the disciples on the day of the Lord's resurrection to be the Spirit of life to them essentially. The same Holy Spirit came upon the disciples on the day of Pentecost to be the Spirit of power economically. As for the Spirit of life, we need to breathe Him in as the breath. As for the Spirit of power, we need to put Him on as the uniform, typified by the mantle of Elijah (2 Kings 2:9, 13-15). The former as the water of life requires our drinking (John 7:37-39); the latter as the water for baptism requires our being immersed. These are the two aspects of the one Spirit for our experience (1 Cor. 12:13). The indwelling of the Spirit of life is essential for our life and living; the outpouring of the Spirit of power is economical for our ministry and work. (*Life-study of Acts*, p. 31)

Further Reading: The Conclusion of the New Testament, msgs. 74-75, 80-81

Enlightenment and inspiration: _____

_____

_____

_____

Morning Nourishment

Matt. ...He Himself will baptize you in the Holy Spirit and
3:11 fire.

Acts And suddenly there was a sound out of heaven, as of
2:2 a rushing violent wind, and it filled the whole house
where they were sitting.

4 And they were all filled with the Holy Spirit and
began to speak in different tongues...

The baptism in the Holy Spirit is the outpouring of the Triune
God, consummated in the all-inclusive compound Spirit, by the
heavenly Head upon His Body on this earth, not for life, but for
administration, not as life essentially, but as power economically
to carry out God's economy. This baptism in the Spirit was proph-
esied by John the Baptist. John told his followers that he was sent
to baptize people in water. To baptize people in water is to termi-
nate people in their old realm of life, the world, and bury them. He
also told his disciples that One was coming after him who would
baptize people in the Spirit (Matt. 3:11). To baptize people in the
Spirit is to bring people into a new realm of life, the kingdom of
God. For the processed Triune God to be given into us as the Spirit
of life is for our germination. Then for the processed Triune God to
be poured upon us as the Spirit of power is to bring us into a new
kingdom. These two things should be put together since they are
both carried out by the same one Spirit (1 Cor. 12:13). (*God's New
Testament Economy,* pp. 98-99)

Today's Reading

The same one Spirit as the Spirit of life germinates us and as
the Spirit of power brings us into a new kingdom. Therefore, all
the believers of Christ are Spirit-germinated persons, and also
persons brought into a new kingdom by the Spirit.

We have to be germinated by the Spirit of life essentially, and
we have to be empowered by the Spirit of power economically.
Then we live God, and we carry out God's plan.

Through the baptism in the Spirit, by being baptized into the
Triune God, the believers were put together to form the Body of

Christ, joined to Him as the Head. Christ is the Head and we are His Body, joined together to be the great universal man. (*God's New Testament Economy,* pp. 99, 103)

The real meaning of the baptism in the Holy Spirit is that we are immersed in God and put God on as our clothing. As Christians and members of Christ, we must be filled with Him inwardly and clothed with Him outwardly. This is what we need, and this is exactly what He is doing with us. We must be clear about this, claim it by faith, and receive it. Then we have it; we are filled within and clothed without, and in this way we are persons who are fully mingled with Him. We can live and walk by Him as life, as power, and as everything. (*A General Sketch of the New Testament in the Light of Christ and the Church, Part 1: The Gospels and the Acts,* p. 65)

The Lord Jesus said in Acts 1:5, "John baptized with water, but you shall be baptized in the Holy Spirit not many days from now." This was accomplished in two sections. First all the Jewish believers were baptized in the Holy Spirit on the day of Pentecost. Then all the Gentile believers were baptized in the house of Cornelius (10:44-47; 11:15-17). In these two sections all genuine believers in Christ have been baptized in the Holy Spirit into one Body once for all universally (1 Cor. 12:13).

Peter's word in Acts 11 proves that what happened in the house of Cornelius was the second step in Christ's baptizing His Body in the Holy Spirit once for all. Peter said, "As I began to speak, the Holy Spirit fell on them just as also on us in the beginning. And I remembered the word of the Lord, how He said, John baptized with water, but you shall be baptized in the Holy Spirit" (vv. 15-16). Therefore,…only these two cases are considered the baptism in the Holy Spirit. In these two instances the Head Himself did something directly on His Body. There was no third party …between the Head and the Body. (*Life-study of Acts,* p. 263)

Further Reading: God's New Testament Economy, chs. 7-8; *Life-study of Acts,* msg. 31

Enlightenment and inspiration: _____

_____

_____

_____

Morning Nourishment

Acts **And as I began to speak, the Holy Spirit fell on**
11:15 **them just as also on us in the beginning.**
  17 **If therefore God has given to them the equal gift as**
       also to us who have believed on the Lord Jesus
       Christ, who was I that I could have forbidden God?
13:9 **But Saul...filled with the Holy Spirit...**

After we have been baptized in the Spirit into one Body, we must drink of the Spirit that we may grow in life and be built up in the Body. To be baptized in the Holy Spirit is to be put into Him, just as to be baptized in water is to be put into it. But to drink of the Holy Spirit is to take Him into us just as to drink water is to take it into us. Baptism is outward and drinking is inward. The outward baptism is for the inward drinking. (*The Baptism in the Holy Spirit*, p. 6)

Today's Reading

The outward aspect of the Holy Spirit's work is mostly included in the baptism in the Holy Spirit. There are five historical cases of the outpouring of the Spirit recorded in Acts. Only two are called the baptism in the Holy Spirit: the outpouring at the day of Pentecost in Acts 2 for the Jewish believers and the outpouring in the house of Cornelius in Acts 10 for the Gentile believers. Acts 1:5 and 11:15-17 verify this fact. In these two instances, Christ as the Head baptized the Jewish and Gentile parts of His Body in the Holy Spirit once and for all. By so doing, He has fully accomplished the baptism in the Holy Spirit upon His entire Body. With the other three cases—(1) the Samaritan believers in Acts 8:17, (2) Saul in Acts 9:17, and (3) the Ephesian believers in Acts 19:6—the Scriptures record the act of the laying on of hands through representative members of the Body. The significance of this act is that the baptism in the Holy Spirit already accomplished upon the Body by the Head was transmitted to the new members of the Body through identification with the Body. The laying on of hands is only a form, of which the real meaning or reality is that we must be rightly related to the Body that we may be in the right position to partake of the baptism in the Holy Spirit already accomplished upon the Body. Therefore, these three cases are not three separate baptisms in the Holy Spirit, but three experiences of the one baptism in the Holy Spirit.

The baptism in the Holy Spirit is uniquely one and was accomplished upon the Body of Christ more than nineteen hundred years ago. But the experiences of the baptism in the Holy Spirit are numerous and continually shared by all the members of the Body of Christ who realize it in this way. We must therefore recognize the one baptism and seek the many experiences of it. Peter first received the baptism (Acts 1:5, 8; 2:4) and later experienced it again and again (4:8, 31).

We must also remember that the baptism in the Holy Spirit is not for life, but for power. It is not the infilling of the Holy Spirit, but the outward aspect of the work of the Holy Spirit. Many Christians and even many Christian teachers confuse the *outward baptism* in the Holy Spirit with the *inward filling* of the Holy Spirit. This is wrong. Two different Greek words are used in the New Testament for these two aspects. One is *pleeroo* for the inward filling; the other is *pleetho* for the outward filling. *Pleeroo* is used in Acts 13:52 and Ephesians 5:18. *Pleerees*, the adjective form of *pleeroo*, is found in Luke 4:1; Acts 6:3, 5; 7:55; and 11:24. These are all instances of the *inward* filling of the Holy Spirit. *Pleetho* is used in Luke 1:15, 41, 67; Acts 2:4; 4:8, 31; 9:17; and 13:9. All these instances are connected with the *outward* filling, the outpouring of the Holy Spirit. Both of these words are used in Acts 2:2-4. The mighty wind *filled (pleeroo)* the house, but the disciples were *filled (pleetho)* with the Holy Spirit. The house was filled inwardly, but the disciples were filled or clothed outwardly. …We should never confuse the inward and outward aspects of the work of the Holy Spirit. The inward is for life; the outward is for power. (*The Baptism in the Holy Spirit,* pp. 6-8)

Further Reading: The Baptism in the Holy Spirit; Life-study of Acts, msgs. 6-8, 30

Enlightenment and inspiration: _____

_____

_____

_____

Morning Nourishment

Acts This Jesus God has raised up, of which we all are
2:32-33 witnesses. Therefore having been exalted to the
right hand of God and having received the promise of the Holy Spirit from the Father, He has
poured out this which you both see and hear.
Eph. And He...gave Him *to be* Head over all things to the
1:22 church.
Acts Then Peter, filled with the Holy Spirit...
4:8

The baptism in the Holy Spirit has already been accomplished, as seen in 1 Corinthians 12:13: "In one Spirit we were
all baptized into one Body, whether Jews or Greeks, whether
slaves or free." Notice that the verb is in the past tense. The
baptism of the whole Body of Christ in the Holy Spirit is...not
to be accomplished in the future or even in the present, but it
has already been accomplished and still exists. It is the same
principle as that which applies for the crucifixion of the Lord
Jesus. If we would believe in Him, we need not ask Him to die
again for us, because His redeeming death has already been
accomplished. It is the same with the baptism in the Holy
Spirit. This baptism has been thoroughly completed upon the
Body and now exists upon the Body, ready for us to take. We
need not ask the Lord to do something again to baptize us in
the Holy Spirit. We have already been baptized by the Lord in
the Holy Spirit in and with the Body. What we need to do now
is simply to take what has already been accomplished! (*The
Baptism in the Holy Spirit,* pp. 8-9)

Today's Reading

We have...given the proper definition of the baptism in the
Holy Spirit. We must now see the proper way to experience it.
First of all, we must realize that the baptism in the Holy Spirit is
an accomplished fact. It is an item of the testament, the will, given
to us all, and we are all entitled to it as members of the Body. However, we must not stop here. We must go on:

(1) We must be right with the Body of Christ and stand in it.

Since the baptism in the Holy Spirit has been accomplished upon the Body of Christ and still exists upon it, we must be properly related to the Body and maintain this proper relationship with the Body in order to be one with it.

(2) We must take the baptism in the Holy Spirit by living faith. If we are right with the Body of Christ, we are in a position to take the baptism in the Holy Spirit. We should realize that it has been already accomplished and now exists upon the Body of Christ. As members of the Body of Christ, maintaining a right relationship with the Body, we are entitled to claim it through the exercise of living faith. (*The Baptism in the Holy Spirit,* pp. 14-15)

On the day of resurrection Christ imparted Himself into His disciples as life, while on the day of Pentecost Christ put all of His disciples into Himself....On the day of resurrection Christ put the "water" into the disciples, while on the day of Pentecost He put the disciples into the "water." This water is Christ, the very Triune God. The Triune God was put into us as our life on the day of resurrection, and we were put into the Triune God on the day of Pentecost. The Triune God is power to us; because we have been put into Him, we have been put into His power and authority. Therefore, within us we have the Triune God as our life, and upon us we have the Triune God as our power and authority.

All of this has been accomplished and applied to us in Christ's resurrection and ascension. Now all we need to do is to receive it by faith. We should simply take it and say amen. If we would say amen to the Lord, we have it.

To get into the Spirit and to take the Spirit into us is to be completely mingled with the Triune God. The Triune God fills and occupies us within, and He covers us without. Within and without, everywhere and in everything, there is the Triune God. (*A General Sketch of the New Testament in the Light of Christ and the Church, Part 1: The Gospels and the Acts,* pp. 86-87, 63)

Further Reading: God's New Testament Economy, chs. 9-10; *Life-study of Acts,* msg. 50; *The Apostles' Teaching,* ch. 2

Enlightenment and inspiration: _____

_____

_____

_____

Hymns, #278

1   The Spirit of life is within us today,
    Who's likened to water our thirst to allay;
    Of Him we may drink and be filled thus with Him,
    Until as a river He flows from within.

2   The Spirit of pow'r comes upon us today,
    Who's likened to clothing ourselves to array;
    In Him we are baptized, with Him we are dressed,
    For service equipping with power possessed.

3   The Spirit of life is as breath glorious,
    As spirit of life it is breathed into us;
    The Spirit of pow'r doth the wind typify,
    Which bloweth upon us with pow'r from on high.

4   Into His disciples the risen Lord breathed,
    The Spirit of life thus to them He bequeathed;
    Th' ascended Lord poured at the Pentecost hour
    Upon His disciples the Spirit of pow'r.

5   The Spirit of life is within as the life,
    The Spirit of power is giv'n for this life;
    As blowing of wind brings the fresh air to breathe,
    The Spirit of power to life doth bequeath.

6   These are not two spirits apart and afar,
    But of the one Spirit the two functions are,
    To clothe us with God and to fill us within,
    That we may be thoroughly mingled with Him.

7   Lord, fill with Thy Spirit of life every part,
    That we may grow up in Thy life as Thou art;
    And clothe us without with Thy Spirit of pow'r
    Thy will to fulfill in Thy service each hour.

Composition for prophecy with main point and sub-points: _____

_____
_____
_____
_____
_____
_____
_____
_____
_____
_____
_____
_____
_____
_____
_____
_____
_____
_____
_____
_____
_____
_____
_____
_____
_____
_____
_____
_____
_____
_____
_____
_____
_____
_____

The Teaching and the Fellowship
of the Apostles

Scripture Reading: Acts 2:42; 1 Tim. 1:3-4; Titus 1:9; 2:1, 7-8;
1 John 1:3

Day 1   I. **The teaching of the apostles is the unique and healthy teaching of God's eternal economy (Acts 2:42; 1 Tim. 1:3-4):**

A. The teaching of the apostles is the entire teaching of the New Testament as God's speaking in the Son to His New Testament people (Heb. 1:1-2):

1. God firstly spoke in the Son as a man in the four Gospels (John 14:10; 5:24; 16:12; 10:30).

2. God secondly spoke in the Son as the Spirit through the apostles in Acts and the twenty-one Epistles (Romans through Jude) (John 16:12-15; Matt. 28:19-20; Heb. 2:3-4; 2 Pet. 3:15-16; Col. 1:25-27).

3. God thirdly spoke in the Son as the seven Spirits through the apostle John in Revelation (1:1-2, 4; 2:1, 7).

Day 2   B. The teaching of the apostles is the unique, divine revelation of God's New Testament economy from the incarnation of God to the consummation of the New Jerusalem—the teaching of the full ministry of Christ in His three divine and mystical stages:

1. The stage of incarnation is for Christ to bring God into man, to unite and mingle God with man, to express God in humanity, and to accomplish His judicial redemption (John 1:14, 29; 5:19; Matt. 1:18, 20).

2. The stage of inclusion is for Christ to be begotten as God's firstborn Son, to become the life-giving Spirit, and to regenerate the believers for His Body (Acts 13:33; 1 Cor. 15:45b; 1 Pet. 1:3).

3. The stage of intensification is for Christ to intensify His organic salvation, to produce the overcomers, and to consummate the New

Jerusalem (Rev. 1:4; 3:1; 4:5; 5:6; 2:7, 17; 3:20; 21:2, 9-10).

C. The teaching of the apostles is the holding factor of the one accord, causing us to have one heart, one way, and one goal (Acts 1:14; 2:42a, 46a; Jer. 32:39).

Day 3

D. Different teachings, other than the teaching of the apostles, are the major source of the church's decline, degradation, and deterioration (1 Tim. 1:3-7; 6:3-5, 20-21a):

    1. The striking point of the churches' degradation is different teachings; these teachings crept in because the churches turned away from Paul's teaching, the unique teaching of God's eternal economy (Rev. 2:14-15, 20; 2 Tim. 1:15).

    2. Different teachings separate us from the genuine appreciation, love, and enjoyment of the precious person of the Lord Jesus Christ Himself as our life and our everything (2 Cor. 11:2-3).

    3. The Lord appreciated the church in Philadelphia because they kept the word, which means that they did not turn away from the healthy teaching of God's economy, the teaching of the apostles (Rev. 3:8; 1 Tim. 6:3).

E. We must be those who are "holding to the faithful word, which is according to the teaching of the apostles" (Titus 1:9):

    1. The churches were established according to the apostles' teaching and followed their teaching, and the order of the churches was maintained by the faithful word, which was given according to the apostles' teaching.

    2. We must speak the things that are fitting to the healthy teaching of the apostles, the teaching of God's economy (2:1, 7-8; 1 Tim. 6:3).

Day 4
&
Day 5

II. **The fellowship of the apostles is the unique and universal fellowship of the Body of Christ— the reality of living in the Body of Christ (Acts 2:42):**

A. Teaching creates fellowship, and fellowship comes

from teaching; if we teach wrongly or differently from the apostles' teaching, our teaching will produce a sectarian, divisive fellowship (1 Cor. 4:17; 1:9; 10:16; 1 Tim. 1:3-4; 6:3).

B. The fellowship is the flow of the eternal life within all the believers, who have received and possess the divine life (1 John 1:3; 2 Cor. 13:14; cf. Rev. 22:1).

C. The initial experience of the apostles was the vertical fellowship with the Father and with His Son, Jesus Christ, but when the apostles reported the eternal life to others, they experienced the horizontal aspect of the divine fellowship (1 John 1:2-3):

1. Our horizontal fellowship with the saints brings us into vertical fellowship with the Lord; then our vertical fellowship with the Lord brings us into horizontal fellowship with the saints (vv. 7, 9).

2. In this divine fellowship God is interwoven with us; this interweaving is the mingling of God and man (cf. Lev. 2:4-5; 1 Cor. 10:17).

Day 6
D. The coordination of the four living creatures presents a beautiful picture of the practical fellowship of the Body of Christ; fellowship means doing everything through the cross and by the Spirit to dispense Christ into others for the sake of His Body (Ezek. 1:5a, 9, 11b-14, 19-22, 25-26; 1 Cor. 12:14-30):

1. The eagle's wings are the means by which the four living creatures are coordinated and move as one, signifying that their coordination is in the divine power, the divine strength, and the divine supply (not in themselves) (Ezek. 1:9, 11; Exo. 19:4; Isa. 40:31; 2 Cor. 12:9; 1 Cor. 15:10).

2. Each of the living creatures faces one direction; as they face these four directions, two of their wings spread out and touch the adjacent creatures' wings, forming a square.

3. When the living creatures move, they do not need to turn; one moves straight forward while

the opposite creature moves backward and the other two move sideways (Ezek. 1:9).

4. In the church service we all need to learn not only how to walk "straight forward" but also how to walk "backward" and "sideways"; in coordination there is no freedom or convenience; coordination keeps us from making turns (cf. Eph. 3:18):

   a. To walk backward and sideways is to say Amen to another member's particular function (or ministry) and burden (Rom. 12:4; cf. 1 Cor. 14:29-31).

   b. If we care only for our particular service and do not have these four kinds of walk, eventually we will become a problem in the church (cf. 3 John 9).

   c. The one who is walking straight forward has the responsibility of following the Spirit (Ezek. 1:12; cf. Acts 16:6-10).

5. If brothers with different functions do not know how to coordinate in fellowship, they will compete and even strive against each other, which could result in division (cf. Phil. 1:17; 2:2; Gal. 5:25-26).

6. Fellowship blends us, mingles us, adjusts us, tempers us, harmonizes us, limits us, protects us, supplies us, and blesses us, giving us the power and the impact of the Spirit; the Body is in the fellowship (1 Cor. 12:24-25; Ezek. 1:13-14).

7. We should apply this matter of coordination not only in a particular local church but also among the churches; this means that we are followers of the churches and that the local churches should fellowship with all the genuine local churches on the whole earth to keep the universal fellowship of the Body of Christ (1 Thes. 2:14; 1 Cor. 10:16).

Morning Nourishment

Heb. **God, having spoken of old in many portions and in**
1:1-2 **many ways to the fathers in the prophets, has at the**
last of these days spoken to us in the Son...
Acts **And they continued steadfastly in the teaching and**
2:42 **the fellowship of the apostles...**

The apostles' teaching is the entire speaking of God in the New Testament. The entire New Testament is the apostles' teaching.

God has spoken, and today God still speaks. There are many matters in God's speaking....Hebrews 1:1-2 says, "God, having spoken of old in many portions and in many ways to the fathers in the prophets, has at the last of these days spoken to us in the Son...." Today God speaks to us in the Son. He does not speak to us in many portions or in many ways, or through the prophets, but...in one person, the Son....The New Testament is very particular. From such a passage we can realize that God's speaking in the New Testament is in the way of incarnation. (*The Apostles' Teaching*, pp. 9-10)

Today's Reading

The incarnation is recorded in the four Gospels. The Jesus who spoke in the four Gospels was the very Son of God, and the Son of God is God Himself. Thus we can say that the Lord Jesus' speaking was God's speaking in the Son as the man in the four Gospels (John 14:10; 5:24; Matt. 28:19-20). John 14:10 says, "Do you not believe that I am in the Father and the Father is in Me? The words that I say to you I do not speak from Myself, but the Father who abides in Me does His works." The Father and the Son are one (John 10:30). When the Son spoke, the Father was speaking. The Father spoke in the person of the Son.

God's speaking did not stop in the four Gospels. He also spoke in the Son as the Spirit through the apostles, from Acts to Revelation (John 16:12-15; Rev. 2:1, 7; 1 Cor. 4:17b; 7:17b; 2 Pet. 3:15-16; Rev. 1:1-2). While God was speaking in the Son, one day the Son told His disciples, "I have yet many things to say to you, but you cannot bear them now. But when He, the Spirit of reality, comes, He will guide you into all the reality; for He will not speak from

Himself, but what He hears He will speak; and He will declare to you the things that are coming. He will glorify Me, for He will receive of Mine and will declare it to you. All that the Father has is Mine; for this reason I have said that He receives of Mine and will declare it to you" (John 16:12-15)....This means that after the four Gospels, there would be God's further speaking.

After the Gospels we have the Acts, where Peter and Paul spoke. Then we have the...[twenty-one Epistles spoken by Paul, James, Peter, John, and Jude]. Finally, we have Revelation, which the Lord Jesus spoke as the Spirit and which was given through John....In chapters two and three of Revelation there are seven epistles. At the beginning of each epistle it is the Lord Jesus who "says." But at the end of each epistle we are told to "hear what the Spirit says to the churches." This indicates that the Lord's speaking was the Spirit's speaking, because He is the Spirit (2 Cor. 3:17). This speaking was written through John. All the epistles written to individual churches were also for all the churches (1 Cor. 4:17b; 7:17b; Col. 4:16). This is God's speaking.

Paul was used by the Lord in his speaking to complete the word of God, especially concerning the mystery of the Triune God (Col. 1:24-25),...but John completed the entire speaking of God....In the book of Revelation God's speaking is fully completed, fully perfected. No one can add anything to it [22:18-19]....Thus, when God speaks today, He simply repeats what He has already spoken.

The teaching of the apostles is the entire speaking of God in the New Testament, first in the Son as a man, then in the Son as the Spirit through the apostles. In the New Testament God cannot depart from the principle of incarnation. He must speak through man. In the four Gospels the man was Jesus. In the succeeding twenty-three books, the men were the apostles. Today we are the men. God speaks in the principle of incarnation. (*The Apostles' Teaching,* pp. 10-13)

Further Reading: The Apostles' Teaching, msg. 1; *The Apostles' Teaching and the New Testament Leadership,* ch. 1

Enlightenment and inspiration: _____

_____

_____

_____

Morning Nourishment

John 1:14 And the Word became flesh and tabernacled among us...

1 Cor. 15:45 ...The last Adam *became* a life-giving Spirit.

Rev. 5:6-7 And I saw...a Lamb standing as having *just* been slain...And He came and took *the scroll* out of the right hand of Him who sits upon the throne.

It is not enough merely to know Christ; we still need to experience and enjoy Him that we may gain Him. To experience, enjoy, and gain Him is not that simple. We can do this only by being in the full ministry of Christ in His three divine and mystical stages....In the first stage, the stage of His incarnation, Christ accomplished four great things. First, He brought God into man; second, He united and mingled God with man; third, He expressed God in His humanity and lived out God's attributes in His human living as His human virtues; and fourth, He accomplished His judicial redemption.

In the second stage of His ministry, the stage of His inclusion, Christ accomplished three great things. First, He was begotten as God's firstborn Son; second, He became the life-giving Spirit; and third, He regenerated the believers for His Body.

In the third stage of His ministry, the stage of His intensification, Christ is accomplishing three great things. First, He is intensifying His organic salvation; second, He is producing His overcomers; and third, He is consummating the New Jerusalem. Hence,...in the three stages of His full ministry, Christ accomplishes ten great things. The New Testament simply deals with these ten things. This is the new language expressing a new culture in the Lord's recovery that has never been seen in Christianity. (*How to Be a Co-worker and an Elder and How to Fulfill Their Obligations*, p. 43)

Today's Reading

The Spirit, who is the biggest factor in the Lord's move in the New Testament today, after the Lord's ascension, is the consummated Spirit, the consummation of the processed and consummated Triune God.

On one side, God's move depends upon Himself as the consummated Spirit. He needs us as the other side so there could be the possibility of accomplishment. If we do not render Him any kind of cooperation or give Him any kind of response, nothing can happen, regardless of how powerful, dynamic, and mighty the Holy Spirit of the Triune God can be. God can do the work of creation by Himself but not the work of the new creation. The new creation work must be carried out in the principle of incarnation, the principle of God being one with man, making one entity out of two elements with no third element produced. The Holy Spirit is the power, the means, and the factor for God's move on this earth, but that is just on one side. There is the need of another side, the human side. There is the need of another factor—the one accord.

The matter of one accord controls the entire revelation concerning the Lord's move on one side. If there were no Spirit on the Lord's side, it would be impossible for the Lord to move on this earth at all. In the same principle, without the one accord on our side, God cannot move. We have to match God. He is now the consummated Spirit, and we have to say, "Lord, we are ready here as the very one accord. We want to not only render but we are also ready to offer to You this one accord." Immediately there is a kind of marriage, and a couple comes out. Then anything can be done.

If you expect to have one accord in any kind of society, group, or movement, you need the same kind of thinking that comes out of the same kind of knowledge....Therefore, Acts tells us that on the one hand, there was one accord among the disciples, and on the other hand, all those who were one in one accord were continuing in the teaching of the apostles (2:42). The teaching of the apostles was the very holding factor of the one accord. If there were more than one teaching, this would damage the holding factor. (*Elders' Training, Book 7: One Accord for the Lord's Move,* pp. 97, 99-100)

Further Reading: How to Be a Co-worker and an Elder and How to Fulfill Their Obligations, ch. 3; Elders' Training, Book 7: One Accord for the Lord's Move, chs. 3, 8

Enlightenment and inspiration: _____

_____
_____
_____

Morning Nourishment

1 Tim. Even as I exhorted you...to remain in Ephesus in
1:3-4 order that you might charge certain ones not to
teach different things nor to give heed to myths and
unending genealogies, which produce questionings
rather than God's economy, which is in faith.
2 Tim. This you know, that all who are in Asia turned away
1:15 from me...

When Paul said that all who were in Asia turned away from
him [2 Tim. 1:15], this does not indicate that they turned away
from the person of Paul because the person of Paul was far away
from them. This verse indicates that they all turned away from
Paul's ministry. Among the churches in Asia was the church in
Ephesus, which was fully established by Paul's ministry as
recorded in Acts 19. They received the gospel, the teaching, the
edification, and the establishment from the ministry of the
apostle Paul. But by the time Paul was imprisoned in Rome, they
had all turned away from his ministry. (*Elders' Training, Book 7:
One Accord for the Lord's Move,* p. 116)

Today's Reading

Paul's second Epistle to Timothy was written about A.D. 68.
About thirty years later, the Lord used John to continue His
divine revelation. The Lord came back to all the churches in Asia
who had turned away from Paul. Because they turned away from
Paul's ministry, the churches in Asia declined into a situation full
of degradation.

[This is why Christianity has become degraded], because they
turned away from the apostle's teaching. Thus, all the different
teachings came in. In 1 Timothy 1:3 and 6:3 Paul warned not to
teach differently. The saints should teach according to Paul's
teaching. Those in Asia definitely turned away from Paul's teaching, and the result of this turning away was that they received
three kinds of heretical teachings. The teaching of Balaam [Rev.
2:14] to worship the idols, the teaching of the Nicolaitans [v. 15] to
build up the hierarchy, even the papal system, and the teaching of

Jezebel [v. 20] to bring the leaven of evil, heretical, and pagan things into the fine flour of Christ (Matt. 13:33) came in because the proper teaching was rejected. Within thirty years after Paul's final Epistle to Timothy, these churches had reached such a point of degradation. It is dangerous to leave or turn away from the apostle's teaching, from the apostle's proper revelation.

The Lord came in these seven epistles to judge those degraded churches. His eyes were as a flame of fire (Rev. 1:14) to observe, search, and enlighten, and out of His mouth proceeded a sharp two-edged sword (1:16), which is His discerning, judging, and slaying word (Heb. 4:12; Eph. 6:17). They turned away from the right word, so the Lord came with this word to judge them. The Lord's feet were like shining brass, as having been fired in a furnace (Rev. 1:15). Brass signifies divine judgment (Exo. 27:1-6). The Lord's coming to the churches in such a way fit in with their turning away from the apostle's teaching and their picking up of different teachings.

One church was unique, and was highly appraised by the Lord—the church in Philadelphia. The Lord highly appraised them and even appreciated them because they [had a little power and] kept the word (Rev. 3:8). That means they did not turn away from the apostle's proper teaching.

To turn away from the proper teaching is a terrible thing that will result in degradation and in picking up other teachings.... I hope we would follow the pattern of the church in Philadelphia—keeping the Lord's word even though we only have a little strength. Let us keep the word of the Lord, which is to remain in the teachings of the apostles, to remain in the healthy words, to remain in the unique revelation from the Lord with the proper leadership. Then we are safe. (*Elders' Training, Book 7: One Accord for the Lord's Move*, pp. 116-118)

Further Reading: The God-ordained Way to Practice the New Testament Economy, chs. 16, 18; Elders' Training, Book 1: The Ministry of the New Testament, chs. 1, 5

Enlightenment and inspiration: _____

_____

_____

_____

Morning Nourishment

Acts **And they continued steadfastly in the teaching and**
2:42 **the fellowship of the apostles, in the breaking of bread**
      and the prayers.
8:17 **Then they [the apostles] laid their hands on them, and**
      they received the Holy Spirit.

Fellowship comes from the teaching. There should be only one unique teaching—the teaching of the apostles. Furthermore, there should be one unique fellowship which is produced by the apostles' teaching. What we teach will produce a kind of fellowship. If we teach wrongly and differently from the apostles' teaching, our teaching will produce a sectarian, divisive fellowship. If I teach baptism by immersion as a condition or a term for receiving the saints, this teaching will produce a Baptist fellowship....Thus, we can see that wrong teaching produces wrong, divisive fellowship. We can have one way for one goal by keeping ourselves strictly in the limit of the apostles' teaching and the apostles' fellowship. There should not be another fellowship besides the apostles' fellowship. (*The God-ordained Way to Practice the New Testament Economy*, p. 153)

Today's Reading

In our work for the Lord, we must keep ourselves in the apostles' fellowship. If you have the burden to go to another locality to have the church life, you should do it with adequate fellowship from the church where you are. If you feel that you can raise up the church life in another city without fellowship with the brothers in the church in your locality, you will be raising up something outside the apostles' fellowship. The apostles' fellowship is universal in time and space. This fellowship includes all parts of the globe and includes all the centuries. Peter, Paul, and all the saints practicing the proper church life were in this fellowship.

The principle of fellowship in the New Testament keeps us living the Body life....As members of the Body of Christ, we should not do things in a detached way....The church in a locality should not be raised up by us independently without any fellowship with the source we came from. By keeping the principle of fellowship, we listen to one another. To listen to one another is to respect the Body....To reject a member of the Body with whom you are connected, is to reject the Body itself. To disregard the Body and not listen to the Body is wrong.

A proper local church is related to other churches. We must remember that there are churches on this earth which are already in existence. The existence of a new church must be related to the churches that are preexisting. To have fellowship with the churches keeps us in the proper fellowship of the apostles, which means that we will be kept in the genuine oneness of the Body of Christ.

We need the balance of no control and no independence. If the saints have the burden to go to raise up the church life, the leading ones should encourage them to do this and help them by giving them warning, advice, and instruction. The believers, on the other hand, should behave and have their entire being kept in fellowship with the existing church to keep them in the unique fellowship of the apostles....In the Body of Christ independence cannot be practiced. Once we practice independence, we get ourselves into the dangerous state of being detached or separated from the Body.

The apostles' fellowship is with the Father and the Son (1 John 1:3) and is also the fellowship of the Spirit (2 Cor. 13:14), which the apostles participated in and ministered to the believers through the preaching of the divine life (1 John 1:2-3). Preaching produces fellowship, and fellowship must be of the divine life....Today in the church, we must realize that if we are going to keep the proper fellowship, we must learn to live by the divine life. When we live by the divine life, we are in...the fellowship. (*The God-ordained Way to Practice the New Testament Economy,* pp. 153-156)

Further Reading: The God-ordained Way to Practice the New Testament Economy, ch. 17; *The Ministry of the New Testament and the Teaching of the Apostles,* ch. 2; *Life-study of Acts,* msg. 12; *A Word of Love to the Co-workers, Elders, Lovers, and Seekers of the Lord,* ch. 4

Enlightenment and inspiration: _____

_____

_____

_____

Morning Nourishment

1 John (And the life was manifested, and we have seen and tes-
1:2-3 tify and report to you the eternal life, which was with
the Father and was manifested to us); that which we
have seen and heard we report also to you that you also
may have fellowship with us, and indeed our fellowship
is with the Father and with His Son Jesus Christ.

In 2 Corinthians 13:14 this divine fellowship is called "the fellowship of the Holy Spirit," in Acts 2:42 it is "the fellowship of the
apostles," and in Philippians 2:1 it is the "fellowship of spirit."
From these portions of the Word, we can see that the divine fellowship belongs to the Father, the Son, the Spirit, the apostles,
and all of the believers. They are all involved in this fellowship.
This divine fellowship involves many persons; hence, it is mutual.
It is impossible for just one person by himself to have this fellowship. The fellowship is one, but it involves many persons.

The fellowship is the flow of the eternal life within all the believers who have received and possess the divine life....By the flow of the
eternal life, the fellowship, all of the believers are kept in oneness.
(*The Triune God to Be Life to the Tripartite Man,* pp. 143-144)

Today's Reading

First John 1:2-3 and 6-7 reveal that the fellowship of the
divine life has both a vertical aspect and a horizontal aspect. The
vertical aspect of fellowship refers to our fellowship with the Triune God. The horizontal aspect of fellowship refers to our fellowship with one another.

[According to] 1 John 1:2-3...the vertical aspect of fellowship
was initially established with the first apostles. The apostles then
reported to sinners the eternal life in order that they might have
fellowship with the apostles. Before the apostles reported the
eternal life to them, the apostles themselves already had the vertical fellowship with the Father and with His Son Jesus Christ
(v. 3). The initial experience of the apostles was vertical, but when
the apostles reported the eternal life to others, they experienced

the horizontal aspect of the divine fellowship.

Verses 6 and 7 of 1 John 1 also indicate the vertical and horizontal aspects of the divine fellowship. Verse 6 says, "If we say that we have fellowship with Him and yet walk in the darkness, we lie and are not practicing the truth." This is the vertical aspect of fellowship. Verse 7 says, "But if we walk in the light as He is in the light, we have fellowship with one another." This is the horizontal aspect of fellowship. Both aspects of the divine fellowship are closely related; therefore, it is difficult to say which aspect comes first. If you do not have the proper fellowship with the Lord, it is difficult to have fellowship with your fellow believers. In the same way, if you do not have the proper fellowship with your fellow believers, it is difficult to have fellowship with the Lord.

Fellowship cannot have just one aspect alone. You cannot have the vertical fellowship without the horizontal fellowship. If you have a good time with the Lord in vertical fellowship, you will be eager to see the other saints in order to have fellowship with them. Once you have fellowship with the saints through prayer, you are brought into vertical fellowship with the Lord again. Your horizontal fellowship with the saints brings you into vertical fellowship with the Lord. Then your fellowship with the Lord brings you into horizontal fellowship with the saints. Thus, these two aspects are always interwoven, that is, they are always crisscrossing each other.

Eventually, in this divine fellowship God is interwoven with us. This interweaving is the mingling of God with man. All of the meetings should be an interwoven fellowship with both the vertical and horizontal aspects. Our married life should also be an interwoven fellowship. The husband and the wife should not only be interwoven with each other but also with the Lord. The real Christian marriage should be the divine fellowship. Our coordination and work together should also be the divine fellowship. (*The Triune God to Be Life to the Tripartite Man,* pp. 144-145, 153, 155)

Further Reading: The Triune God to Be Life to the Tripartite Man, msgs. 17-18; *A Brief Presentation of the Lord's Recovery,* pp. 35-43

Enlightenment and inspiration: _____

_____
_____
_____

Morning Nourishment

Ezek. ...And this was [the four living creatures'] appear-
1:5-6 ance: They had the likeness of a man. And every one
had four faces, and every one of them had four wings.
   9 Their wings were joined one to another; they did not
turn as they went; each went straight forward.
  12 ...Wherever the Spirit was to go, they went; they did
not turn as they went.

In order to be harmonized, blended, adjusted, mingled, and
tempered in the Body life, we have to go through the cross and be
by the Spirit, dispensing Christ to others for the sake of the Body
of Christ. The co-workers and elders must learn to be crossed out.
Whatever we do should be by the Spirit to dispense Christ. Also,
what we do should not be for our interest and according to our
taste but for the church. As long as we practice these points, we
will have the blending.

All of these points mean that we should fellowship. When a
co-worker does anything, he should fellowship with the other co-
workers. An elder should fellowship with the other elders. Fellowship tempers us; fellowship adjusts us; fellowship harmonizes us;
and fellowship mingles us. We should forget about whether we
are slow or quick and just fellowship with others. We should not
do anything without fellowshipping with the other saints who are
coordinating with us. Fellowship requires us to stop when we are
about to do something. In our coordination in the church life, in
the Lord's work, we all have to learn not to do anything without
fellowship. (*The Divine and Mystical Realm,* p. 87)

Today's Reading

The four living creatures [in Ezekiel 1] are coordinated. Each
of the living creatures faces one direction, respectively facing
north, south, east, and west. As they face these four directions,
two of their wings spread out and touch the adjacent creatures'
wings, forming a square. Each of the living creatures uses two of
his wings to join with other living creatures.

[According to] verse 12,...every one of the living creatures goes straight forward. They do not turn, but some return, that is, move backward....Thus, one goes straight forward while the opposite creature moves backward. At the same time, the other two living creatures must move sideways....No matter in which direction the living creatures are moving, there is no need for any one of them to turn....This is a beautiful picture of the coordination that we need in the church life.

Coordination keeps us from making turns. If one is moving by himself, he may first move to the north and then turn and move to the east. Later he may turn again to move to the south and eventually turn once more and move to the west. He moves in many directions by making many turns. In the Lord's ministry, on the contrary, there is no such turning. Instead, one moves straight forward, and those who coordinate with him move either backward or sideways.

We all need to keep our position and go straight forward. We also need to learn to walk backward and sideways, saying "Amen" to another's position, function, and ministry. This means that in the church life we all need to learn to have four kinds of walk: the straight forward walk, the backward walk, the sideways walk to the right, and the sideways walk to the left. If we do not learn to have these four kinds of walk, we will become a problem to our local church. The more we grow, learn, function, and minister, the more trouble we will cause because we know only how to walk forward and to have turns.

We should apply this matter of coordination not only in a particular local church but also among the churches. This means that we should be followers of the churches (1 Thes. 2:14). We are one Body in one move of the Lord. When one church takes the lead in a definite direction under the leading of the Holy Spirit, we all should walk backward and sideways to follow. (*Life-study of Ezekiel,* pp. 68-69, 72, 78)

Further Reading: Life-study of Ezekiel, msgs. 7-8, 10; *The Divine and Mystical Realm,* ch. 6

Enlightenment and inspiration: _____

_____

_____

_____

Hymns, #1285

1   The faith which once for all was giv'n
    Unto the saints of old,
    Has been committed unto us
    To guard, defend, and hold.

> And we know whom we have believèd
> And are persuaded that He is able
> To guard, through the Holy Spirit,
> Our deposit to that day.

2   This good deposit is the mark
    Of God's economy,
    Without it we will miss the aim
    Of His recovery.

3   The myst'ry of the common faith,
    A conscience pure requires;
    A holy, separated life
    For us the Lord desires.

4   This outline of the healthy words,
    In faith and love we'll hold;
    All different teaching, fruitless talk,
    Reject with spirit bold.

5   Oh, healthful teaching, wholesome words:
    The truth of godliness!
    Oh, good deposit, common faith,
    And life of holiness!

6   Lord, make us now those faithful men
    Who pass on what we've heard;
    Make us examples of the saints
    In spirit, faith, and word.

Composition for prophecy with main point and sub-points: _____

_____

_____

_____

_____

_____

_____

_____

_____

_____

_____

_____

_____

_____

_____

_____

_____

_____

_____

_____

_____

_____

_____

_____

_____

_____

_____

_____

_____

_____

_____

_____

_____

_____

_____

_____

The Heavenly Vision
and Vanquishing Conversion
of the Apostle Paul

Scripture Reading: Acts 9:1-19; 22:6-16; 26:13-19

Day 1 **I. The heavenly vision of Paul's completing ministry must be seen by us, and this vision must be renewed in us day by day (Acts 26:19; Eph. 1:17; Prov. 29:18a):**

A. This vision of the age will keep us living in God's presence; this vision will uphold us, control us, and become our divine commission to meet the need of this age (Jer. 1:7-10, 18-19; Isa. 6:1-8; Acts 26:16-19).

B. When we see a vision of God's plan and have been converted from everything to Christ Himself, He will be the inner operating God to us, energizing us to carry out His plan (Gal. 1:15-16; Rom. 15:16; 1 Cor. 15:10; Phil. 2:13; cf. Jer. 1:1, 4-10, 18-19).

C. Eventually, the opposing Saul became, in his victorious ministry of the gospel, Christ's vanquished captive in the triumphal procession celebrating Christ's victory over all His enemies; the Lord's perfecting of His chosen vessels in such a way is excellent and marvelous (Acts 26:14; 2 Cor. 2:14; Eph. 4:7-12).

Day 2 **II. While Saul of Tarsus was on the way to Damascus, a heavenly vision came to him, and this vision revolutionized him (Acts 9:1-19; 22:6-16; 26:13-19):**

A. After he saw the vision, he became blind, unable to see anything, and impotent, unable to do anything; a blessed blindness comes upon those who are met by the heavenly vision:

1. After this blindness comes upon us, there will be the inner anointing and the inner shining, the inner enlightening; we, who were once God's enemies, will be brought into the feast of the New Testament ministry to be

saved in Christ's life (v. 14; Rom. 5:10; 1 Cor. 5:8; cf. 2 Kings 6:18-23).

2. The inner vision will increase more and more and will revolutionize the way that we serve the Lord; this vision will control us to do everything by the Spirit, in our spirit, and in the Body, through the Body, and for the Body (Gal. 5:25; Phil. 3:3; Rom. 1:9; 1 Cor. 12:12, 27).

B. For three days Saul did not see anything, and he did not eat or drink anything; all he could do was pray (Acts 9:9, 11):

1. Under the inspiration of the essential Spirit, his only interest was to pray in order to know the significance of what he had seen and heard (22:14-15).

2. It is likely that as Saul was praying, vision after vision and revelation after revelation came to him concerning Christ as the embodiment of God, the mystery of God, and the church as the Body of Christ, the mystery of Christ (Col. 2:2; Eph. 3:4; 5:32).

3. Each crucial point of Paul's vision recorded in Acts 9 should not merely be a teaching to us but a vision that we see on the heavenly "television."

C. In our reading of Acts 9 we need to see the heavenly vision concerning three items—"Me" (v. 4), "Jesus" (v. 5), and the "chosen vessel" (v. 15).

Day 3 III. **"Saul, Saul, why are you persecuting Me?" (v. 4):**

A. This is a corporate "Me," comprising Jesus the Lord and all His believers; He is the Head, and we are His Body as one person, one new man (Eph. 2:15; Col. 3:10-11).

B. Saul (who is also Paul) began to see that the Lord Jesus and His believers are one great person— the wonderful "Me"; to him this was a unique revelation in the entire universe (Acts 13:9a; 1 Cor. 12:12-27; Eph. 3:3-4; 5:32).

C. Paul is the only writer of the New Testament to use the term *the Body of Christ;* he placed great emphasis on the Body because at the time of his conversion he heard a message concerning the corporate "Me," a message concerning the Body of Christ (Rom. 12:4-5; 1 Cor. 12:12-27; Eph. 1:22-23; 2:16; 4:4, 16).

D. Immediately after Saul was saved, the Lord began to educate him concerning the Body of Christ; those who see that they are members of the Body treasure the Body and honor the other members (Acts 9:6, 17-18, 24-25; 1 Cor. 12:23-24; 16:18).

Day 4 IV. **"Who are You, Lord? And He said, I am Jesus, whom you persecute" (Acts 9:5):**

A. *Lord* here equals the word *Jehovah* in Hebrew (Exo. 3:14-15; John 8:58).

B. The name *Jesus* embodies the full message of the gospel; Paul saw that Jesus is Jehovah the Savior and that as the One who is now in the heavens, He has passed through the process of incarnation, human living, death, resurrection, and ascension for the producing and building up of the Body of Christ (Rom. 9:5; Eph. 1:19-23).

C. Paul saw that Jesus is the very God, Jehovah, who has been processed and consummated with the divine and human elements to be the ascended Lord, the Head of the Body, and the life-giving Spirit, the Spirit of Jesus, to be dispensed into all His members (Rom. 10:12-13; Col. 1:18a; 1 Cor. 15:45b; Acts 16:7; Phil. 1:19).

D. Paul saw that the center of the universe is that Christ is in us and we are in Christ; he saw that God's plan is both to reveal Christ in us as life so that we may live Christ and to put us into Christ so that we may be conformed to His image and built up with others to be His living Body for His corporate expression (Gal. 1:15-16; 2:20; 4:19; Rom. 8:28-29; 12:1-5; Eph. 1:22-23; 3:16-19).

Day 5 V. **"This man is a chosen vessel to Me" (Acts 9:15):**

A. God's intention in saving Saul of Tarsus was to fill him with Himself and thereby make him an outstanding vessel (Col. 1:25; Eph. 3:8-9).

B. Paul's writings develop the spiritual significance of the word *vessel:*

    1. Paul saw that man is a tripartite vessel to contain and be filled with Christ as life for the building up of the Body of Christ (Gen. 2:7; 1 Thes. 5:23-24; Rom. 9:21, 23; 2 Cor. 4:7; 2 Tim. 2:20-21; cf. 2 Kings 4:1-6; Jer. 48:11).

    2. The Body of Christ is God's great corporate vessel to contain Him and be filled with Him for His expression (Eph. 3:16-19).

C. As God's chosen vessel, Paul was converted from everything to Christ Himself—converted to call on His name, to suffer on behalf of His name, and to bear His name before both the Gentiles and kings and the sons of Israel (Acts 9:14-16; 22:16).

Day 6 **VI. The central vision of the apostle Paul's completing ministry is God in us as our contents ("vessel"), Christ as the mystery of God ("Jesus"), and the church as the mystery of Christ ("Me") (9:4-5, 15):**

A. Paul's preaching in Acts and his writing in his Epistles are a detailed description of the heavenly vision seen by him (26:16; 22:15; Eph. 3:3-6).

B. The Lord appeared to Paul to appoint him as a minister and a witness both of the things in which Paul had seen Him and of the things in which He would appear to Paul (Acts 26:16; cf. 1:8; 23:11; 20:20, 31).

C. In all the visions that Paul saw, he saw Christ; the things in which we have seen Christ and the things in which He will appear to us are the things that we must minister to others (Gal. 1:15-16; Acts 22:14-15).

VII. The Lord's recovery today is the recovery of the central vision of Paul's completing ministry (26:13-19; Col. 1:25; Eph. 5:32).

Morning Nourishment

Phil. **But what things were gains to me, these I have**
3:7-8 **counted as loss on account of Christ. But moreover**
       I also count all things to be loss on account of the
       excellency of the knowledge of Christ Jesus my Lord
       ...that I may gain Christ.

[Philippians 3:5-7 reveals Paul's life] before his conversion and his attitude after his conversion. What was this young man converted from? We think a man is always converted from sin to God because man is sinful and has fallen away from God. According to the Scriptures, however, Saul was converted from religion to Christ,...not merely from sin to God.

You may have been regenerated, but maybe even today you need a real, practical conversion from the traditional things, from the religious things, unto the living Christ. A person can only be regenerated once. But in my experience I can testify that I have had a number of conversions. Regeneration is once for all, but conversion, to have some change in your life, is not just once for all. (*A Young Man in God's Plan,* pp. 25-26)

Today's Reading

I was born in Christianity, and I was taught and raised up in Christianity. But when I was nineteen years old, I was regenerated, and that was my first conversion. A real change in life transpired inwardly. Not long after I had been regenerated, I began to meet with a group of Christians who paid much attention to the teachings, to the knowledge of the Bible. I stayed with them for seven and a half years....[Then], one day the Lord gave me another conversion, another change. He opened my eyes to see that the Christian life is not a matter of merely dealing with the knowledge of the Bible or with doctrine, but a matter of dealing with Christ as the living One. That brought about a great change in my life....To be a Christian is not a matter of knowledge,...of just studying the Bible in letters, ...but a matter of dealing with the living Christ as our life.

After I learned how to experience Christ as life and how to deal with this living Christ, the Lord really gave me the burden for the work. I worked diligently, heartily, and even fruitfully. I worked and worked day and night, day after day. But one day the Lord intervened and stopped me from the work....This was another conversion experience for me. I absolutely had no ability to work due to a serious illness I contracted. I was kept absolutely away from the work by the Lord for nearly two and a half years. In that time I was converted from the work to the Lord Himself.

We need a conversion not necessarily from anything sinful or evil, but from good things, from religious things, from substitutes for Christ Himself, which prevent Him from occupying, filling, saturating, permeating, and possessing our entire inward being. ...We need many conversions from everything other than the living Christ Himself.

After I was saved, I loved to study the Word....I would take the Bible to bed with me so I could look at it as soon as I awoke in the morning. Eventually, this love to study the Word became something taking the ground of Christ in my life. I loved the study of the Word much more than Christ Himself....Eventually and sovereignly, the Lord intervened and now I dare not study the Word in that way. I was also very fond of teaching the Scriptures.... Even this matter can become something between you and the Lord Himself. Now I am careful not to go beyond what the Lord is speaking in me (2 Cor. 13:3) and what He needs me to speak.

There could be many things in our life which take the place of the Lord Himself. My burden is to fellowship with you and help you to realize that God's plan is to work Christ Himself into you (Gal. 1:16; 2:20; 4:19). This is God's goal, His ultimate intention....You need to be converted all the time from something other than Christ to Christ Himself. Whenever anything becomes a hindrance between you and Christ, you have to be converted from that to Christ Himself. (*A Young Man in God's Plan,* pp. 26-29)

Further Reading: A Young Man in God's Plan, ch. 3; *Life-study of Acts,* msg. 25; *The Perfecting of the Saints and the Building Up of the House of God,* ch. 9

Enlightenment and inspiration: _____

_____

_____

_____

Morning Nourishment

Acts ...**Suddenly a light from heaven flashed around
9:3-4 him. And he fell on the ground and heard a voice...
8-9 And Saul rose from the ground; and though his eyes
were open, he could see nothing. And they led him
by the hand...And he was three days without seeing, and he neither ate nor drank.**

A heavenly vision came to [Paul on the way to Damascus].
This vision turned him, changed him, revolutionized him (Acts
9:1-5)....After he saw this vision, he became blind and very weak,
even impotent. Before this vision came to him, Paul was clear, full
of sight, and he was also potent, able to do many things. But
suddenly a heavenly vision came to him, and Paul was changed.
He became blind, unable to see anything, and impotent, unable to
do anything. Before the vision came to him, he took the lead to do
things, but after the vision came, he needed others to guide him.

There needs to be a time in our Christian life when we realize
that we are blind, when we realize that our sight is gone and that
we do not know the direction but need others to lead us. It is a
blessing to be blind in this way. Oh, blessed blindness! If you have
never had a time in your Christian life when you became blind
and impotent, then your service to God will be like Paul's service
before he got saved. Those who serve in this way will be clear
about everything and will have the full assurance that they are
doing the right thing and that they know the right way to go on.
But a blessed blindness comes upon those who are met by the
heavenly vision. After this blindness comes upon us, there will be
the inner anointing and the inner shining, the inner enlightening.
The inner vision will increase more and more and will revolutionize the way we serve the Lord. In serving the Lord we will become
a different person. (*The Heavenly Vision,* pp. 8-9)

Today's Reading

Acts 9:9 says that Saul "was three days without seeing, and he
neither ate nor drank." What did he do during those three days?
...In verse 11 [the Lord says to Ananias]: "Rise up and go to the

lane called Straight, and seek in the house of Judas a man from Tarsus named Saul; for behold, he is praying." Here we see that in those three days Saul was praying. He did not see anything, and he did not eat or drink anything. All he could do was pray.

I believe that as Saul prayed he tried to analyze Jesus, seeking to know who He is.

It is likely that as Saul was praying, vision after vision and revelation after revelation came to him concerning Christ and the church. His experience during those days may have been one of watching a heavenly television in which he saw many things concerning the Lord Jesus. As he saw these things, Saul may have said, "Jesus the Nazarene is Jehovah. He is my Savior. No wonder that His followers testified strongly that He was resurrected. He surely has been resurrected, for He appeared to me from the heavens." Saul may have gone on to consider the Lord's ascension, which implies His incarnation, human living, death, and resurrection. Saul may have come to realize that as the One who is now in the heavens, the Lord passed through the process of incarnation, human living, death, resurrection, and ascension.

We need to be impressed with the fact that for three days Saul did not eat or drink. All he did was pray. While he was praying, the revelation concerning Christ was "televised" into his being. Saul beheld a wonderful view of the Lord on this heavenly television. No longer did Saul have any doubt concerning Christ's resurrection. He also came to believe in His incarnation and death. Through the visions that he saw during those days, Saul received the full message of the gospel.

According to 9:5, Saul said, "Who are You, Lord? And He said, I am Jesus, whom you persecute." The "Me" in verse 4 and the name "Jesus" in verse 5 are of great significance, and [during those three days] Paul must have considered much concerning Jesus and this corporate "Me." (*Life-study of Acts,* pp. 211-213)

Further Reading: Life-study of Acts, msg. 26; *The Heavenly Vision,* chs. 1, 3; *Life–study of 1 & 2 Kings,* msg. 14

Enlightenment and inspiration: _____

_____
_____
_____

Morning Nourishment

Acts ...Saul, Saul, why are you persecuting Me? And he
9:4-6 said, Who are You, Lord? And He *said,* I am Jesus,
    whom you persecute. But rise up and enter into the
    city, and it will be told to you what you must do.
  17 ...And laying his hands on him, he said, Saul,
    brother, the Lord has sent me...so that you may
    receive your sight and be filled with the Holy Spirit.

Saul not only saw that Jesus is Jehovah, the Savior, who died
and was resurrected; he also saw that the Lord Jesus is one with
His followers....In this way Saul came to see the Body....When
the Lord appeared to Saul, He asked him, "Why are you persecuting Me?" [Acts 9:4]. The Lord seemed to be saying, "Saul, this 'Me'
includes Me personally and My Body corporately. Personally I am
in the heavens, but corporately the Body is on earth. When you
persecuted My followers, you persecuted My Body. To persecute
My Body is to persecute Me." Therefore, the "Me" in verse 4 is corporate, comprising the Lord Jesus and all His believers.

Saul's experience of the corporate Me, Christ and the Body,
must have made a deep impression on him and affected his future
ministry regarding Christ and the church. That experience laid
the foundation for his ministry. Therefore, he was very strong in
teaching the Body of Christ (Rom. 12:4-5; 1 Cor. 12:12-27; Eph.
1:22-23; 2:16; 4:4, 16). He is the only writer in the New Testament
to use the term "the Body of Christ." He placed great emphasis on
the Body because at the time of his conversion he heard a
message concerning the corporate Me, a message concerning the
Body of Christ. (*Life-study of Acts,* pp. 212-214)

Today's Reading

Immediately after Saul was saved, the Lord began to educate
him concerning the Body. This was the reason He said to Saul,
"Rise up and enter into the city, and it will be told to you what you
must do" (Acts 9:6). Here the Lord seemed to be saying, "Saul, I
shall not tell you what you need to do. You have been saved
directly by Me, and no other person knows that you have been

saved. Therefore, you need a representative of My Body to come to you and confirm the fact that I have saved you, chosen you, and called you. You also need such a representative of the Body to bring you into the identification with My Body."

[The Lord sent Ananias] to contact Saul. In his contact with Saul, Ananias recognized him as a brother in the Lord (v. 17). If the Lord had not told Ananias to seek out Saul, none of the believers would have recognized Saul as a brother. Through Ananias the Lord gave Saul excellent instruction concerning the practice of the Body life.

In Acts 9:17 Ananias said to Saul, "The Lord has sent me— Jesus, who appeared to you on the road on which you were coming—so that you may receive your sight and be filled with the Holy Spirit." The filling here is the outward filling with the economical Spirit. Both in the case of Saul in chapter nine and in the case of the Samaritans in chapter eight, the Head of the Body withheld the economical Spirit.

Saul was a leading persecutor of the church....Who would ever believe that he had turned to the Lord and had been saved? When Paul received the Lord's salvation, he also received the essential Spirit within him. However, the Head of the Body held back the economical Spirit until a representative of the Body came to Saul and laid his hands on him. At that juncture, the economical Spirit came upon him as strong evidence of the fact that he had been saved and had been accepted by the Head into the Body as a member. (*Life-study of Acts,* pp. 214-215)

If we realize that a Christian is nothing more than a member, we will no longer be proud. Everything depends on our seeing. Those who see that they are members will surely treasure the Body and honor the other members. They will not see just their own virtues; they will readily see others as being better than themselves. (*The Mystery of Christ,* p. 17)

Further Reading: Life-study of Acts, msg. 26; *The Mystery of Christ,*
　　msgs. 2-3

Enlightenment and inspiration: _____

_____

_____

_____

Morning Nourishment

Gal. 1:15-16	But when it pleased God, who set me apart from my mother's womb and called me through His grace, to reveal His Son in me that I might announce Him as the gospel among the Gentiles...
Col. 1:25-26	...I became a minister according to the stewardship of God, which was given to me for you, to complete the word of God, the mystery...

Saul of Tarsus was one of a strong character. He was happily nearing the end of his journey from Jerusalem to Damascus, eager to arrive and fulfill his task of arresting all those who believed in Jesus. It was midday as he approached Damascus. Suddenly "a great light flashed out of heaven around" him (Acts 22:6). He fell to the ground and heard a voice saying, "Saul, Saul, why are you persecuting Me?" (v. 7). He must have thought, "What do you mean? I have been persecuting Peter, and John, and Stephen. But all those whom I have persecuted were on the earth. I have never harmed anyone in the heavens. Who can this be, saying that I am persecuting him?"

So he asked. Calling this unseen One Lord, he said, "Who are You, Lord?" (v. 8). The answer came, "I am Jesus!" Saul must have been filled with consternation. Jesus was crucified and buried. How could He be speaking from the heavens? How could He be alive?

Such was the calling of Paul. All mysterious! (*The Completing Ministry of Paul*, p. 2)

Today's Reading

Why was the Lord after Saul? The Lord needed an apostle to complete His revelation. There may be many preachings, but they do not adequately complete God's revelation. The purpose of Paul's calling was to get the one person who could complete that revelation (Col. 1:25).

Without Paul's ministry, what would we lack?...What would we be missing? Firstly, we would not realize that Christ is in us, that He must live in us and be our life and life supply. In the other forty-three books this point is not clearly stressed. Of course, John's Gospel mentions that we must abide in Him and He in us (John 15:4) and that because He lives, we also shall live (14:19). Without Paul's writings, however, these words would not be easy to understand. It is Paul who tells us that Christ must live in us, must live in our spirit, and be in us as the life-giving Spirit. He is our life, even our life supply, and is Himself to be formed in us.

Secondly, Paul's writings reveal Christ as the all-inclusive One. No other books of the Bible reveal Christ as the embodiment of God, as the Firstborn of all creation, as the Firstborn from among the dead, and as the reality of all positive things.

Thirdly, only in Paul's writings do we find Christ as the Head and the church as the Body. This thought was not there before Paul's ministry. It is his Epistles which develop this truth.

These three points are the completion of God's revelation. Because of Paul's writings, we know that Christ in us is the hope of glory, that Christ is the all-inclusive One, and that the church is the Body and Christ the Head.

In Saul's thinking, Jesus of Nazareth was a man on this earth who had been crucified and buried. To his astonishment this very One came to him from the heavens! Here is a further indication that Christ is all-inclusive. Not only are all His disciples included in Him. He is also present everywhere. He is on the earth, but He is also in the heavens.

The Lord's words, "Why do you persecute Me?" caused Saul to realize that the believers were one with Christ. Saul may have thought, "I have not been persecuting anyone in the heavens," but the Lord was indicating to him that those whom he had been persecuting were members of His Body. Because they were one with Him, for Saul to touch them was to touch the Head. (*The Completing Ministry of Paul,* pp. 3-4, 7)

Further Reading: A Young Man in God's Plan, ch. 2; *The Completing Ministry of Paul,* msg. 1

Enlightenment and inspiration: _____

_____
_____
_____

Morning Nourishment

Acts   …This man is a chosen vessel to Me, to bear My name
9:15   before both the Gentiles and kings and the sons of
       Israel.
Rom.   In order that He might make known the riches of His
9:23   glory upon vessels of mercy, which He had before pre-
       pared unto glory.
Eph.   …That you may be filled unto all the fullness of God.
3:19

In Acts 9:15 we see that Saul of Tarsus was a chosen vessel. In reading the Scriptures we may not pay adequate attention to the word "vessel," an important spiritual term. A vessel is a container and therefore is different from a tool or a weapon.

In the Epistles of Paul there is a strong emphasis on the importance of vessels.…Romans 9:23 speaks of God making known "the riches of His glory upon vessels of mercy, which He had before prepared unto glory." In Romans 9 we have the thought that human beings were made by God to be vessels to contain Him. In 2 Corinthians 4:7 Paul again speaks of vessels: "We have this treasure in earthen vessels that the excellency of the power may be of God and not out of us." Then in 2 Timothy 2:20 he says, "In a great house there are not only gold and silver vessels but also wooden and earthen; and some are unto honor, and some unto dishonor."

Saul of Tarsus was chosen by the Lord not only to be His apostle, His servant, and His minister; he was also chosen to be His vessel. In Acts 9:15 the Lord Jesus seemed to be saying to Ananias, "Saul is a chosen vessel. He will contain Me, and his ministry will be to convey Me to the Gentile world." We all need to see the importance of Saul being a chosen vessel. (*Life-study of Acts*, pp. 216-217)

Today's Reading

[Consider two bottles.] The purpose of these bottles is to contain some kind of beverage. One bottle may be dirty and the other may be clean, but the bottles were not made merely to be clean. They were made to be filled with a certain beverage. In like manner, God does not merely desire to have many "clean people." What

God wants to have is many people filled with Christ. He does not want religious people but Christians. A Christian is a Christ-man, a man filled with Christ, a man mingled with Christ, a man lost in Christ. All over the world, it is relatively easy to meet Christians, but it is not so easy to meet some Christians who are filled with Christ and whose goal is Christ Himself. It is possible to meet many working Christians, religious Christians, and active Christians who act for Christ, yet it is not so easy to meet some Christians who are one with Christ, filled with Christ, and occupied solely by Christ.

I have the impression that many may be working for a religious system just like Saul of Tarsus worked for Judaism. You may be working for religion and have nothing to do with Christ. I hope that the Lord has opened our eyes to see that God's plan is to reveal His Son in us so that we can be conformed to the image of His Son. God's intention and God's plan is not for us to be religious, good, spiritual, or knowledgeable of the Scriptures, but God's plan is for us to be filled with Christ, to be occupied, possessed, saturated, permeated, blended, and mingled with Christ. This is why Paul tells us in Philippians 3:7-8, "But what things were gains to me, these I have counted as loss on account of Christ. But moreover I also count all things to be loss on account of the excellency of the knowledge of Christ Jesus my Lord, on account of whom I have suffered the loss of all things and count them as refuse that I may gain Christ." Paul was brought to the realization that the only gain in the universe was Christ Himself. To him Christ was the one reality of all. Nothing was real to him but Christ.

God's plan is to work Christ into us, so throughout our life we need many conversions. Whenever there is something in your life substituting for Christ, you need a conversion from that very thing to Christ Himself. We should always keep ourselves in direct contact with Christ. Then we will be one with Christ in reality. (*A Young Man in God's Plan,* pp. 29-30, 32)

Further Reading: A Young Man in God's Plan, ch. 3

Enlightenment and inspiration: _____

_____

_____

_____

Morning Nourishment

Acts   ...I have appeared to you for this *purpose*, to
26:16 appoint you as a minister and a witness both of the
       things in which you have seen Me and of the things
       in which I will appear to you.
   19 Therefore, King Agrippa, I was not disobedient to
       the heavenly vision.

The central vision of the apostle Paul's completing ministry is: God in us as our contents, Christ as the mystery of God, and the church as the mystery of Christ. We must lay aside our natural concepts whether religious, ethical, devotional, or spiritual, holy, or pious. Even the concept of having a good meeting or a strong service must not be our goal. The meetings and the service must come from the source; the church life is the issue.

The Lord's recovery is the central vision. In 1970, after the successful migrations, we began to pay attention to the spread of the recovery and became somewhat negligent of the central vision. The recovery was off, for which I have very much repented to the Lord. By His mercy He cleared things up and brought us back to the right track. The Lord has rebuked me and charged me not to do much to encourage the spreading of the recovery or to gain an increase in numbers....Let the recovery grow in life. Spontaneously there will be a spreading and a proper increase, both issuing from life, not from our doing. "Little one," the Lord pointed out, "when I was on the earth, I didn't do anything to spread my work. All I did was to sow Myself as life into a small number. Eventually in Acts 1, I had only one hundred twenty. Not many." It seems unbelievable that after the Lord's labors for three and a half years all that He reaped was a mere one hundred twenty. The Lord asked me, "From all your efforts to spread and increase, where are the one hundred twenty? After you go, where are the one hundred twenty? Who will carry on the Lord's recovery on the right track?" (*The Completing Ministry of Paul*, pp. 95-96)

Today's Reading

We need some faithful ones to rise up and say, "Lord, here I am.

Show me the central vision as you did with the apostle Paul." I hope you younger ones, especially those who are in their twenties, will do this. Then after ten years you will be valuable to the Lord's recovery.

There is only one writer in the Bible who tells us of the Body of Christ. The Old Testament writers saw nothing of it. It was a mystery hidden from them. The mystery of Christ, which is His Body, has been made manifest only in the New Testament age. Yet only Paul refers to it. Peter does not. Nor does John, even though his mending ministry was to bring the saints back to Paul's completing ministry. Even in Paul's writings, only four of his fourteen Epistles speak of the Body of Christ; the other ten do not mention it. Romans, 1 Corinthians, Ephesians, and Colossians are the only books that refer to the Body of Christ....Paul received a unique vision that the church is the Body of Christ.

Even to have a communal life based on Acts 2:44-45 is not the Body....By Acts 6 the communal life was almost over because of the murmurings. Then Paul came on the scene. He told the Corinthians to bring their offerings to the church meetings on the Lord's Day to take care of others (1 Cor. 16:1-2). Here is a strong indication that communal living was at an end. There may be a communal life without the Body of Christ. A communal life can be set up, but not so with the Body of Christ. The Body requires the resurrection, ascension, and headship of Christ.

Our God today is in us to be our contents. The mystery of God is Christ as the embodiment and manifestation of God, making God so real and so enjoyable to us. The mystery of Christ is that the Triune God through death and in resurrection is mingling Himself with us, making us the living members of His organic Body. This vision must direct us. It will keep us in the central lane, walking according to the mingled spirit and being in the Body life. This is what the Lord is after. (*The Completing Ministry of Paul,* pp. 96, 103-104, 107)

Further Reading: The Completing Ministry of Paul, chs. 11-12

Enlightenment and inspiration: _____

_____

_____

Hymns, #513

1   Once it was the blessing,
     Now it is the Lord;
   Once it was the feeling,
     Now it is His Word;
   Once His gift I wanted,
     Now, the Giver own;
   Once I sought for healing,
     Now Himself alone.

     All in all forever,
       Only Christ I'll sing;
     Everything is in Christ,
       And Christ is everything.

2   Once 'twas painful trying,
     Now 'tis perfect trust;
   Once a half salvation,
     Now the uttermost;
   Once 'twas ceaseless holding,
     Now He holds me fast;
   Once 'twas constant drifting,
     Now my anchor's cast.

3   Once 'twas busy planning,
     Now 'tis trustful prayer;
   Once 'twas anxious caring,
     Now He has the care;
   Once 'twas what I wanted,
     Now what Jesus says;
   Once 'twas constant asking,
     Now 'tis ceaseless praise.

4   Once it was my working,
     His it hence shall be;
   Once I tried to use Him,
     Now He uses me;
   Once the pow'r I wanted,
     Now the Mighty One;
   Once for self I labored,
     Now for Him alone.

5   Once I hoped in Jesus,
        Now I know He's mine;
     Once my lamps were dying,
        Now they brightly shine;
     Once for death I waited,
        Now His coming hail;
     And my hopes are anchored
        Safe within the veil.

Composition for prophecy with main point and sub-points: _____

_____

_____

_____

_____

_____

_____

_____

_____

_____

_____

_____

_____

_____

_____

_____

_____

_____

_____

_____

_____

_____

_____

_____

_____

_____

_____

_____

God's Central Testimony—
the Incarnated, Crucified,
Resurrected, and Ascended Christ
as the All-inclusive One

Scripture Reading: Acts 2:22-36; 3:13-15, 22-23, 26; 4:10-12; 5:30-31; 9:20, 22; 13:33-34

Day 1

I. As we study the book of Acts, we need to have the view of the Lord Jesus as the One who is on the throne economically and within us essentially; this is the revelation that precedes the book of Acts (Heb. 12:2; Rev. 5:6; 2 Tim. 4:22; 1 Cor. 6:17).

II. God's central testimony is the incarnated, crucified, resurrected, and ascended Christ (Acts 1:3, 9-11; 2:22-24, 32-36).

III. We all need the full enjoyment of Christ as the Feast of Harvest; this full enjoyment of Christ is actually the all-inclusive life-giving Spirit as the consummation of the processed Triune God reaching us (v. 1, footnote 1).

IV. All the apostles carried out the same ministry to bear the testimony of the incarnated, crucified, resurrected, and ascended Jesus Christ, who is Lord of all, announcing Christ in His person and work (1:17; 9:20, 22; 10:36-43):

Day 2

A. With Christ there are two main aspects—the aspect of His person and the aspect of His work; *the Son of God* denotes His person, and *the Christ* denotes His work (9:20, 22; John 20:31):

1. For the Lord Jesus to be the Son of God means that He is God, the One with the unique divine source (1:18; 3:16).

2. For the Lord Jesus to be the Christ means that He is the God-anointed and God-appointed One to carry out whatever God intends (Matt. 16:16-18).

B. Peter witnessed concerning the man Jesus in His

work, death, resurrection, and ascension (Acts 2:22-36):

Day 3
1. While Christ was living and ministering, whatever He did was an exhibition that His work was done by God and was fully tested, proved, and approved by God (v. 22).
2. The Lord's crucifixion was not an accident in human history but a purposeful fulfillment of the divine counsel determined by God, taking place according to the eternal predestination of the Triune God (v. 23).
3. Christ's resurrection was God's approval and declaration of Him as the real Messiah, the One anointed and appointed by God to carry out His eternal commission (vv. 24-32).
4. Christ's ascension was God's exaltation of Him; the pouring out of the Holy Spirit was a proof that God had exalted the Lord Jesus and made Him both Lord and Christ (vv. 33-36).

C. Jesus' incarnation made Him a man, His human living on earth qualified Him to be man's Savior, His crucifixion accomplished full redemption for man, His resurrection vindicated His redemptive work, and His exaltation inaugurated Him to be the ruling Leader that He might be the Savior; this exalting of Him was the ultimate step in His being perfected to be the Savior of man (5:30-31; Heb. 2:10; 5:9).

Day 4
V. **The apostles' testimony of Jesus Christ, the Lord of all, was all-inclusive; as depicted in the book of Acts, they preached and ministered the all-inclusive Christ (3:13-26; 4:10-12; 13:22-39):**

A. In his ministry Peter announced the all-inclusive Christ (3:13-26; 4:10-12):
1. The Lord Jesus, the Servant of God, the Healer, is *the holy and righteous One* (3:13-14, 16):
   a. As the holy One, He is absolutely for God, unto God, and one with God.

Day 5

Day 6

     b. As the righteous One, He is right with God and with everyone and everything (v. 14).

2. Christ is the Author of life, the origin and Originator of life, the Chief Leader in life (v. 15).

3. The Lord Jesus is the Prophet, who speaks for God and speaks forth God (vv. 22-23).

4. Christ is the seasons of refreshing; to have Christ is to have times of refreshing (v. 20).

5. Christ is the seed in whom we receive God's blessing (v. 25).

6. God's way of sending the ascended Christ was by pouring out the Spirit; when the outpoured Spirit came to the people, that was Christ, the ascended One, sent by God to them (v. 26).

7. As the Stone-Savior, Christ is the material for God's building; in resurrection God made Him the cornerstone, the prominent stone that joins the walls of a building (4:10-12).

B. In his ministry Paul announced the all-inclusive Christ; he carried out a work of presenting, conveying, and ministering the all-inclusive Christ realized as the life-giving Spirit (13:22-39; 1 Cor. 15:45b):

1. Through resurrection Christ became the firstborn Son of God; God's raising up Jesus from the dead was His begetting of Him to be His firstborn Son (Acts 13:33; Rom. 8:29):

     a. As the only begotten Son, the Lord is the embodiment of the divine life (John 1:4; 1 John 5:11-12).

     b. As the firstborn Son, Christ is the life-dispenser for the propagation of life (Rom. 1:3-4; 8:2, 6, 10-11, 29).

     c. In Acts 13 Paul was preaching Christ as the firstborn Son for propagation; for this reason, he preached the resurrection of the Lord Jesus as His birth in His humanity to be God's firstborn Son (v. 33).

2. The resurrected Christ is a great gift given by God to us, and this gift is entitled *the holy things of David, the faithful things* (v. 34):
   a. This Holy One is Christ, the Son of David, in whom God's mercies are centered and conveyed; hence, *the holy things of David, the faithful things* refers to the resurrected Christ.
   b. The holy and faithful things are all the aspects of what Christ is—Christ Himself as mercies to us, an all-inclusive gift given by God to us for our experience and enjoyment (v. 34).

Morning Nourishment

Acts This Jesus God has raised up, of which we all are
2:32-33 witnesses. Therefore having been exalted to the
right hand of God and having received the promise of the Holy Spirit from the Father, He has
poured out this which you both see and hear.
36 ...God has made Him both Lord and Christ, this
Jesus whom you have crucified.

Many of today's Christians do not realize that our Savior is
both the essential One and the economical One. As the essential
One, He dwells within us. But as the economical One, He is sitting
in heaven. We have quoted the line of the hymn that says, "Lo! in
heaven Jesus sitting." The Lord Jesus is sitting in heaven not essentially but economically. Simultaneously, He is within us essentially. How wonderful! This is the revelation that precedes the book of
Acts.

We need to see this revelation as we come to Acts. This means
that as we study Acts we need to have the view of the Lord Jesus
as the One who is on the throne economically and within us
essentially. (*Life-study of Acts*, p. 8)

Today's Reading

It is not my burden in this life-study of Acts to cover all the
minor points contained in this long book. For example, I am not
burdened to speak on such a matter as David being a man according to God's heart. Rather, my burden in this life-study is to cover
all the crucial points regarding God's New Testament economy.

Acts is not merely concerned with acts. This is a book showing
us God's dispensation, God's economy, God's arrangement in His
eternal economy.

Wonders and signs are not part of God's central testimony of
the incarnated, crucified, resurrected, and ascended Christ; neither are they part of His full salvation. Rather, signs and wonders
are only evidences that what the apostles preached and ministered was absolutely of God, not of man.

Many Christians do not realize that Christ secretly ascended to the Father early in the morning on the day of His resurrection. Of course, He ascended openly forty days later. On the day of His resurrection the Lord went to the heavens to offer Himself as the first-fruits of God's harvest for the satisfaction of God the Father. That was a secret ascension. The day of Pentecost was fifty days later.

As we have pointed out, the Feast of Pentecost was the fulfill-ment of the Feast of Weeks, which was also called the Feast of Harvest. The Feast of Harvest typifies the enjoyment of the rich produce brought in by the resurrected Christ. Not many readers of the Bible pay adequate attention to the fact that Pentecost actually refers to the harvest and that the harvest typifies the enjoyment of all the riches of the resurrected Christ. This rich produce is actually the all-inclusive Spirit.

After enjoying Christ as the firstfruits, the disciples went on to enjoy Him as the harvest on the day of Pentecost. To enjoy the essential Spirit is to have the enjoyment as the sheaf of the firstfruits. But to enjoy the economical Spirit is to have the enjoy-ment of Christ as the harvest in an open, public way.

We should not neglect the enjoyment of Christ as the harvest. Some may want to be like Mary, who met with the Lord on the morning of His resurrection, or at least like the disciples, who met with Him in the evening. We all need the full enjoyment of Christ as the Feast of Harvest.

Speaking of Judas, Peter goes on to say in Acts 1:17, "For he was numbered among us and was allotted his portion of this min-istry." This ministry, mentioned also in verse 25, is the ministry to bear the testimony of Jesus (v. 8). Though the apostles were twelve in number, their ministry was uniquely one—this minis-try, a corporate ministry in the principle of the Body of Christ. All the apostles carried out the same ministry to bear the testimony not of any religion, doctrine, or practice, but uniquely of the incar-nated, resurrected, and ascended Jesus Christ, the Lord of all. (*Life-study of Acts,* pp. 331-332, 47, 49, 40)

Further Reading: Life-study of Acts, msgs. 1, 5-6

Enlightenment and inspiration: _____

_____

_____

_____

Morning Nourishment

Acts **And immediately he [Saul] proclaimed Jesus in**
9:20 **the synagogues, that this One is the Son of God.**
 22 **...And he [Saul] confounded the Jews dwelling in**
      Damascus by proving that this One is the Christ.
John **But these have been written that you may believe**
20:31 **that Jesus is the Christ, the Son of God, and that**
      believing, you may have life in His name.

With the all-inclusive Christ there are two main aspects—
the aspect of His person and the aspect of His work. We see
these two aspects in Acts 9:20 and 22, where Saul speaks of
the Son of God and the Christ. The Son of God denotes the
Lord's person, and the Christ denotes His work.

As the Son of God, the Lord Jesus is the divine One, even the
very God Himself....John 5:18 says, "Because of this therefore the
Jews sought all the more to kill Him, because He...called God
His own Father, making Himself equal with God." This indicates
that for the Lord to be the Son of God means that He is God.

The expression "the Son of God" refers to the person of the
Lord Jesus. As the Son of God, the Lord Jesus is divine.
However, all the opposers considered Him merely a human
being. They did not realize that this Jesus is also divine, that
He is the Son of God. He is the One with the unique divine
source. (*Life-study of Acts,* p. 220)

Today's Reading

According to Acts 9:22, Saul proved to the Jews in Damascus
that "this One is the Christ." The title "the Christ" denotes the
Lord's commission, that is, the Lord's work. Christ means the anointed One. The Lord Jesus is God's anointed One. As the anointed
One of God, the Christ, He is the unique One. Only He has been
anointed by God and appointed by Him to carry out His commission, to do work God assigned to Him.

In Matthew 16:15 the Lord Jesus said to His disciples, "Who
do you say that I am?" Simon Peter answered and said, "You are
the Christ, the Son of the living God" (v. 16). The revelation given

to Peter includes the two aspects of the Lord Jesus, the aspects of His person and His commission. Christ's commission is to accomplish God's eternal purpose through His crucifixion, resurrection, ascension, and second coming. His person embodies the Father and issues in the Spirit for a full expression of the Triune God.

Saul of Tarsus...received a heavenly vision concerning the Lord Jesus. He saw the same thing Peter did in Caesarea Philippi; that is, he saw that Jesus the Nazarene is the Son of God and the Christ.

The Lord Jesus is both human and divine. As a divine-human person, He is the God-man. The Lord is the One with a dual status—human and divine. In Acts 9 Saul does not emphasize the Lord's humanity, for everyone, including the opposers, recognized that Jesus was a human being and not a phantom. He was truly a man, and His humanity was recognized by all. But the opposers did not see that Jesus is the Son of God. Therefore, immediately after Saul turned to the Lord, the first thing he testified concerning Him is that Jesus, the man from Nazareth, is the Son of God. As we have pointed out, this was blasphemy to the Jews, and they wanted to do away with Saul for proclaiming it.

In addition to proclaiming that Jesus is the Son of God, Saul also testified that He is the Christ. He is unique, the only One anointed and appointed by God to carry out God's commission.

In 2:22-36 Peter witnesses of the man Jesus in His work, death, resurrection, and ascension. In verse 36 Peter declares, "Therefore let all the house of Israel know assuredly that God has made Him both Lord and Christ, this Jesus whom you have crucified." Jesus was made the Lord to possess all, and He was made the Christ to carry out God's commission. As God, the Lord Jesus was already the Lord, and in His divinity there was no need for Him to be made Lord. Nevertheless, in His ascension He, as a man, was made the Lord of all by God. God made Jesus the Lord of all to possess all things, including us. (*Life-study of Acts,* pp. 221-222, 83)

Further Reading: Life-study of Acts, msg. 27; *The Conclusion of the New Testament,* msgs. 21, 75

Enlightenment and inspiration: _____

_____

_____

_____

Morning Nourishment

Acts This man, delivered up by the determined counsel
2:23-24 and foreknowledge of God, you, through the hand of
lawless men, nailed to *a cross* and killed; whom God
has raised up, having loosed the pangs of death,
since it was not possible for Him to be held by it.

In Acts 2:22 Peter says, "Men of Israel, hear these words: Jesus the Nazarene, a man shown by God to you to be approved by works of power and wonders and signs, which God did through Him in your midst, even as you yourselves know." The first message of the apostles' preaching of the gospel is focused on a Man whom Luke in his Gospel presented to his readers from His conception through His birth, youth, life on earth, death, and resurrection, to His ascension. Now Luke's succeeding narrative goes on to tell us that this Man was preached by the apostles as the God-ordained Savior.

The Greek word translated "shown" in verse 22... indicates that the Lord's work was God's demonstration of Him, His exhibition of Him. While Christ was living and ministering, whatever He did was an exhibition of the fact that His work was done by God. In the four Gospels we have the exhibition of a wonderful Person, the God-man. The Gospels exhibit this God-man as the One who was fully tested, proved, and approved. Peter's thought in verse 22 is that Jesus was fully tested, proved, and approved by God. (*Life-study of Acts,* pp. 75-76)

Today's Reading

In Acts 2:23 we see that the Lord's death was according to God's determined counsel and foreknowledge....This determined counsel must be a counsel held by the Trinity before the foundation of the world (1 Pet. 1:20; Rev. 13:8). This indicates that the Lord's crucifixion was not an accident in human history, but a purposeful fulfillment of the divine counsel determined by the Triune God.

This was done according to God's eternal purpose and plan, not accidentally. Hence, in the eternal view of God, from the foundation of the world, that is, the fall of man as a part of the world, Christ was slain (Rev. 13:8).

In Acts 2:24-32 Peter speaks concerning the resurrection of the Lord Jesus. His resurrection was God's approval of Him to be the Messiah. Through the resurrection of Christ God was declaring that the resurrected Christ was the real Messiah, the One anointed and appointed by God to carry out His eternal commission.

Christ's ascension was God's exaltation of Him. In exalting Christ, God made Him both Lord and Christ. The pouring out of the Holy Spirit is a proof that God has exalted the Lord Jesus and has made Him both Lord and Christ.

Acts 2:33 says, "Therefore having been exalted to the right hand of God and having received the promise of the Holy Spirit from the Father, He has poured out this which you both see and hear." This is not the promise given by the Lord in John 14:16-17 and 15:26, but the promise given by the Father in Joel 2:28, quoted by Peter in Acts 2:17, and referred to by the Lord in Luke 24:49 and Acts 1:4, concerning the Holy Spirit. The exalted Christ's receiving of the promise of the Holy Spirit is actually the receiving of the Holy Spirit Himself. Christ was conceived of the Spirit essentially for His being in humanity (Luke 1:35; Matt. 1:18, 20), and He was anointed with the Spirit economically for His ministry among men (Matt. 3:16; Luke 4:18). After His resurrection and ascension, He still needed to receive the Spirit economically again so that He might pour Himself out upon His Body to carry out on earth His heavenly ministry for the accomplishment of God's New Testament economy. (*Life-study of Acts,* pp. 76-77, 79-80)

Jesus' incarnation made Him a man, His human living on earth qualified Him to be man's Savior, His crucifixion accomplished full redemption for man, His resurrection vindicated His redemptive work, and His exaltation inaugurated Him to be the ruling Leader that He might be the Savior. This exalting of Him was the ultimate step in His being perfected to be the Savior of man (Heb. 2:10; 5:9). (Acts 5:31, footnote 1)

Further Reading: Life-study of Acts, msg. 10; *The Conclusion of the New Testament,* msg. 16

Enlightenment and inspiration: _____

_____
_____
_____

Morning Nourishment

Acts But you denied the holy and righteous One and
3:14-15 asked that a man *who was* a murderer be granted
to you; and the Author of life you killed, whom God
has raised from the dead, of which we are witnesses.

The Lord's resurrection is the focus of the apostles' testimony.
It refers back to His incarnation, humanity, human living on
earth, and God-ordained death (Acts 2:23), and points forward
to His ascension, ministry and administration in heaven, and
coming back. Thus the apostles' testimony of Jesus Christ, the
Lord of all, is all-inclusive, as depicted in the whole book of
Acts. They preached and ministered the all-inclusive Christ as
revealed in the entire Scriptures. (*Life-study of Acts*, p. 40)

Today's Reading

In Acts 3:14 Peter said to the people, "But you denied the holy
and righteous One and asked that a man who was a murderer be
granted to you."…In this verse "holy" indicates that Jesus, the
Nazarene, the One despised by the Jewish leaders, was absolutely for God and separated unto Him. Furthermore, He was
absolutely one with God. According to the denotation of the word
"holy" in the Bible, it signifies one who is absolutely unto God, who
is absolutely for God, and who is absolutely one with God. In all of
human history only the Lord Jesus is such a One. David was good,
but at least in one instance he was for himself and not for God.
However, throughout His entire life the Lord Jesus was absolutely separated unto God, for God, and one with God. There was
never an instant when He was not absolutely for God and one
with Him. Therefore, He is called the holy One. He alone deserves
the title "the Holy One."

According to 3:14, Peter called the Lord Jesus not only the holy
One but also the righteous One. To be righteous is to be right with
God and also with every one and with every thing. Only the Lord
Jesus can be called the righteous One, because only He is right
with God and with everyone and with everything. In ourselves we

are not right with God, with others, or even with things. For example, in anger we may kick a door or knock over a chair. This is to be wrong with the door or the chair. We, therefore, cannot be the righteous One.

In 3:15 Peter went on to say, "And the Author of life you killed, whom God has raised from the dead, of which we are witnesses." Here the Greek word rendered "Author" is *archegos*, meaning author, origin, originator, chief leader, captain. It denotes Christ as the origin or Originator of life, hence, the Author of life, in contrast to the murderer in the previous verse.

In this verse the King James Version has "the Prince of life." This is a poor rendering. In 3:15 *archegos* does not denote a prince; it denotes the very source, origin, even originator, of life, the Author of life. Here Peter is saying that the Healer is the source of life, the Originator of life; He is the Author, the Chief Leader, in life. Peter was indicating that the Healer is not merely a Healer—He is the source, origin, and Initiator of life.

What we have in chapter three of Acts is not merely a matter of healing. Here we see the imparting of life into others. This is to propagate Christ. For such a propagation, we need the Lord as the Author of life, as the source of life.

In 3:22 and 23 Peter indicates that the Lord Jesus is the Prophet....Therefore, in this chapter we see that the Lord Jesus is the Servant, the Holy One, the righteous One, the Author of life, and the Prophet.

In 3:19-20 Peter said to the Jews, "Repent therefore and turn, that your sins may be wiped away, so that seasons of refreshing may come from the presence of the Lord."

The seasons of refreshing are times of cooling, reviving, relieving. Have you ever entered into such a season of refreshing?... Actually, every proper conversion is a season of refreshing....To some extent, we all have experienced this....The season of refreshing is Christ Himself. (*Life-study of Acts*, pp. 102-107)

Further Reading: Life-study of Acts, msgs. 13-14

Enlightenment and inspiration: _____

_____

_____

_____

Morning Nourishment

Acts **This is the stone which was considered as nothing**
4:11-12 **by you, the builders, which has become the head of**
the corner. And there is salvation in no other, for
neither is there another name under heaven given
among men in which we must be saved.

Peter utters a concluding word in Acts 3:26: "To you first, God, having raised up His Servant, has sent Him to bless you in turning each of you away from your wicked deeds." God has sent back the ascended Christ to the Jews first by pouring out His Spirit on the day of Pentecost. Hence, the Spirit God poured out is the very Christ God raised and exalted to the heavens. When the apostles preached and ministered this Christ, the Spirit was ministered to people.

Actually, God has received Christ into the heavens. But here Peter says that God has sent this ascended One to the people.... God sent Him by pouring out the Spirit. That was God's way of sending the ascended Christ to the people. This implies that the outpoured Spirit is actually the ascended Christ Himself. When the outpoured Spirit came to the people, that was Christ, the ascended One, sent by God to them. From this we see that the poured-out Spirit is identical to the ascended Christ. In God's economy for the experience of His people, the ascended Christ and the poured-out Spirit are one. In God's economy Christ and the Spirit are one for our enjoyment. (*Life-study of Acts,* p. 114)

Today's Reading

In Acts 4 Peter was given the opportunity to present this Healer in a further way, presenting Him as a stone for God's building.

God came in incarnation to be a stone for the building up of His universal habitation, but the Jewish leaders, who should have been the builders, despised this stone. However, God made Him the cornerstone. The more the Jewish leaders rejected Him, the more God used Him. First, He was a stone only in a general way. But after the rejection by the Jewish leaders, God in resurrection made Him the cornerstone. At first He was a common stone. Then Jewish leaders rejected Him by killing Him. But God honored Him by raising Him up from among the dead and making Him a particular stone, the cornerstone, the very prominent stone that joins the walls of a building. Christ is the cornerstone of God's habitation.

Because he was under the leading of the Holy Spirit and the regulation of the Spirit of Jesus, Paul carried on a work of presenting, conveying, and ministering the all-inclusive Christ to others. Paul did not minister law, genealogies, prophecies, or types—he ministered the living and all-inclusive Christ.

Beginning with Acts 13:30, Paul went on to speak of Christ's resurrection: "But God raised Him from the dead."

After pointing out that the resurrected Christ "appeared to those who had come up with Him from Galilee to Jerusalem, who are now His witnesses to the people" (v. 31), Paul went on to say, "We announce to you the gospel of the promise made to the fathers, that God has fully fulfilled this promise to us their children in raising up Jesus, as it is also written in the second Psalm, 'You are My Son; this day have I begotten You.'" Resurrection was a birth to the Man Jesus. He was begotten by God in His resurrection to be the firstborn Son of God among many brothers (Rom. 8:29). He was the only begotten Son of God from eternity (John 1:18; 3:16). After incarnation, through resurrection, He was begotten by God in His humanity to be God's firstborn Son.

This means that Christ's resurrection was His birth as the firstborn Son of God. Jesus, the Son of Man, was born to be the Son of God through being raised up from the dead. Therefore, God's raising up of Jesus from the dead was His begetting of Him to be His firstborn Son. We need to realize that the Lord's resurrection was His birth. This is a crucial matter. (*Life-study of Acts,* pp. 127-128, 395, 318-319)

Further Reading: Life-study of Acts, msgs. 15-16, 36

Enlightenment and inspiration: _____

_____
_____
_____

Morning Nourishment

Acts   That God has fully fulfilled this *promise* to us their
13:33-34 children in raising up Jesus, as it is also written in
          the second Psalm, "You are My Son; this day have I
          begotten You." And as to His having raised Him up
          from the dead, no longer to return to corruption, He
          spoke in this way, "I will give you the holy things of
          David, the faithful things."

As the only begotten Son of God, the Lord is the embodiment of the divine life...(John 1:4). Through resurrection Christ became the firstborn Son of God as the life-dispenser for the propagation of life. First, He was the only begotten Son as the embodiment of life; now He is the firstborn Son for the propagation of life. Through His becoming the firstborn Son of God in resurrection, the divine life has been dispensed into all of His believers to bring forth the propagation of the very life which is embodied in Him.

Here in Acts 13 Paul was not preaching Christ as the only begotten Son of God, as the Gospel of John does. Rather, here Paul was preaching Christ as the firstborn Son of God for propagation. For this reason, he preached the resurrection of the Lord Jesus as His second birth. Through His second birth, His birth in resurrection, Christ became the firstborn Son of God for the propagation of the divine life. (*Life-study of Acts,* p. 320)

Today's Reading

In Acts 13:34 Paul speaks a further word regarding the resurrection of Christ....The words "the holy things of David, the faithful things" has bothered translators of the New Testament. Verses 33 and 34 are concerned with the resurrected Christ.... [According to verse 33], Christ's resurrection was His second birth to bring Him forth as the firstborn Son of God. God promised to give Him to His people, and this resurrected One is the holy and faithful things of David. The words "the holy things of David, the faithful things" indicates that Christ was of David, for it was out of David's seed that God raised up such a One. To God, the resurrected Christ is the firstborn Son, but to us He is the Savior. Moreover, He is a great gift given by God to His chosen people, and this gift is entitled "the holy and faithful things."

Literally, the Greek words rendered "the holy things, the faithful things" are the holy things (Gk. *hosios,* plural), the faithful or sure. The same word *(hosios)* is used for "Holy One" in the next verse, but in the singular. But it is not the regular word for holy, which is *hagios. Hosios* is a Greek equivalent of the Hebrew word *chesed,* which is translated "mercies" in Isaiah 55:3; 2 Chronicles 6:42; and Psalm 89:1, both in the Septuagint and in the King James Version. In Psalm 89 *chesed* in verse 1 for mercies in plural is the same word in verse 19 for Holy One in singular. This Holy One is Christ, the Son of David, in whom God's mercies are centered and conveyed. Hence, the holy and faithful things of David refer to the resurrected Christ. This is fully proved by the context, especially by "Your Holy One" in the following verse (Acts 13:35), and by the verse following Isaiah 55:3.

The resurrected Christ, who is God's firstborn Son brought forth through His second birth, His resurrection, is the holy and faithful things. In Acts 13:34 the word "faithful" means trustworthy.

What are these holy and trustworthy things? They are all the aspects of what Christ is. According to the New Testament, Christ is life, light, grace, righteousness, holiness, sanctification, and justification. He is also the bread of life and the living water. Furthermore, the holy and trustworthy things include all the aspects of Christ unveiled in 1 Corinthians: power, wisdom, righteousness, sanctification, redemption, glory, the depths of God, the unique foundation of God's building, the Passover, the unleavened bread, the spiritual food, the spiritual drink, the spiritual rock, the Head, the Body, the firstfruits, the second Man, and the last Adam.... Oh, how much Christ is to us as the holy and trustworthy things! (*Life-study of Acts,* pp. 321-323)

Further Reading: Life-study of Acts, msgs. 37-38; *The Conclusion of the New Testament,* msg. 38

Enlightenment and inspiration: _____

_____

_____

_____

Hymns, #199

1 Thou art the Rock everlasting,
   Spiritual Rock cleft for me;
   Drinking of Thee as the Spirit,
   Thus I become one with Thee.
   Thou art the Rock never shaken,
   'Tis on this Rock we are built;
   Joined unto Thee thru redemption,
   Nothing can shake us thru guilt.

   Lord, how we treasure Thy value,
   All that Thou art is for us;
   While here in loving remembrance
   We share Thy wealth glorious.

2 Thou art the Stone tried by many,
   Precious to God, dear to us,
   Thou art so sure and trustworthy,
   Thy strength is so marvelous.
   Thou art the Stone that is living,
   Chosen of God, made our own;
   So energetic and pow'rful,
   With endless life to us known.

3 Thou art the Stone of Foundation
   Laid by our God, safe and sure;
   It is by this sure foundation
   Safety fore'er we secure.
   To us no other foundation
   Of any kind man can lay;
   Thou art the only foundation
   Which we have now and for aye.

4 Lord, for God's spiritual building,
   Thou art the Chief Cornerstone;
   Both of the Jews and the Gentiles
   By Thee are built into one.
   Lord, Thou art also the Topstone,
   Brought forth in measureless grace;
   Thou art our cover and glory,
   Moving our hearts in Thy praise.

Composition for prophecy with main point and sub-points: _____

_____
_____
_____
_____
_____
_____
_____
_____
_____
_____
_____
_____
_____
_____
_____
_____
_____
_____
_____
_____
_____
_____
_____
_____
_____
_____
_____
_____
_____
_____
_____
_____
_____
_____
_____

Wk.	Lord's Day	Monday	Tuesday	Wednesday	Thursday	Friday	Saturday
1	☐ Gen 1:1-5	☐ 1:6-23	☐ 1:24-31	☐ 2:1-9	☐ 2:10-25	☐ 3:1-13	☐ 3:14-24
2	☐ 4:1-26	☐ 5:1-32	☐ 6:1-22	☐ 7:1—8:3	☐ 8:4-22	☐ 9:1-29	☐ 10:1-32
3	☐ 11:1-32	☐ 12:1-20	☐ 13:1-18	☐ 14:1-24	☐ 15:1-21	☐ 16:1-16	☐ 17:1-27
4	☐ 18:1-33	☐ 19:1-38	☐ 20:1-18	☐ 21:1-34	☐ 22:1-24	☐ 23:1—24:27	☐ 24:28-67
5	☐ 25:1-34	☐ 26:1-35	☐ 27:1-46	☐ 28:1-22	☐ 29:1-35	☐ 30:1-43	☐ 31:1-55
6	☐ 32:1-32	☐ 33:1—34:31	☐ 35:1-29	☐ 36:1-43	☐ 37:1-36	☐ 38:1—39:23	☐ 40:1—41:13
7	☐ 41:14-57	☐ 42:1-38	☐ 43:1-34	☐ 44:1-34	☐ 45:1-28	☐ 46:1-34	☐ 47:1-31
8	☐ 48:1-22	☐ 49:1-15	☐ 49:16-33	☐ 50:1-26	☐ Exo 1:1-22	☐ 2:1-25	☐ 3:1-22
9	☐ 4:1-31	☐ 5:1-23	☐ 6:1-30	☐ 7:1-25	☐ 8:1-32	☐ 9:1-35	☐ 10:1-29
10	☐ 11:1-10	☐ 12:1-14	☐ 12:15-36	☐ 12:37-51	☐ 13:1-22	☐ 14:1-31	☐ 15:1-27
11	☐ 16:1-36	☐ 17:1-16	☐ 18:1-27	☐ 19:1-25	☐ 20:1-26	☐ 21:1-36	☐ 22:1-31
12	☐ 23:1-33	☐ 24:1-18	☐ 25:1-22	☐ 25:23-40	☐ 26:1-14	☐ 26:15-37	☐ 27:1-21
13	☐ 28:1-21	☐ 28:22-43	☐ 29:1-21	☐ 29:22-46	☐ 30:1-10	☐ 30:11-38	☐ 31:1-17
14	☐ 31:18—32:35	☐ 33:1-23	☐ 34:1-35	☐ 35:1-35	☐ 36:1-38	☐ 37:1-29	☐ 38:1-31
15	☐ 39:1-43	☐ 40:1-38	☐ Lev 1:1-17	☐ 2:1-16	☐ 3:1-17	☐ 4:1-35	☐ 5:1-19
16	☐ 6:1-30	☐ 7:1-38	☐ 8:1-36	☐ 9:1-24	☐ 10:1-20	☐ 11:1-47	☐ 12:1-8
17	☐ 13:1-28	☐ 13:29-59	☐ 14:1-18	☐ 14:19-32	☐ 14:33-57	☐ 15:1-33	☐ 16:1-17
18	☐ 16:18-34	☐ 17:1-16	☐ 18:1-30	☐ 19:1-37	☐ 20:1-27	☐ 21:1-24	☐ 22:1-33
19	☐ 23:1-22	☐ 23:23-44	☐ 24:1-23	☐ 25:1-23	☐ 25:24-55	☐ 26:1-24	☐ 26:25-46
20	☐ 27:1-34	☐ Num 1:1-54	☐ 2:1-34	☐ 3:1-51	☐ 4:1-49	☐ 5:1-31	☐ 6:1-27
21	☐ 7:1-41	☐ 7:42-88	☐ 7:89—8:26	☐ 9:1-23	☐ 10:1-36	☐ 11:1-35	☐ 12:1—13:33
22	☐ 14:1-45	☐ 15:1-41	☐ 16:1-50	☐ 17:1—18:7	☐ 18:8-32	☐ 19:1-22	☐ 20:1-29
23	☐ 21:1-35	☐ 22:1-41	☐ 23:1-30	☐ 24:1-25	☐ 25:1-18	☐ 26:1-65	☐ 27:1-23
24	☐ 28:1-31	☐ 29:1-40	☐ 30:1—31:24	☐ 31:25-54	☐ 32:1-42	☐ 33:1-56	☐ 34:1-29
25	☐ 35:1-34	☐ 36:1-13	☐ Deut 1:1-46	☐ 2:1-37	☐ 3:1-29	☐ 4:1-49	☐ 5:1-33
26	☐ 6:1—7:26	☐ 8:1-20	☐ 9:1-29	☐ 10:1-22	☐ 11:1-32	☐ 12:1—14:21	☐ 13:1—14:21

Reading Schedule for the Recovery Version of the Old Testament with Footnotes

Wk.	Lord's Day	Monday	Tuesday	Wednesday	Thursday	Friday	Saturday
27	☐ 14:22—15:23	☐ 16:1-22	☐ 17:1—18:8	☐ 18:9—19:21	☐ 20:1—21:17	☐ 21:18—22:30	☐ 23:1-25
28	☐ 24:1-22	☐ 25:1-19	☐ 26:1-19	☐ 27:1-26	☐ 28:1-68	☐ 29:1-29	☐ 30:1—31:29
29	☐ 31:30—32:52	☐ 33:1-29	☐ 34:1-12	☐ Josh 1:1-18	☐ 2:1-24	☐ 3:1-17	☐ 4:1-24
30	☐ 5:1-15	☐ 6:1-27	☐ 7:1-26	☐ 8:1-35	☐ 9:1-27	☐ 10:1-43	☐ 11:1—12:24
31	☐ 13:1-33	☐ 14:1—15:63	☐ 16:1—18:28	☐ 19:1-51	☐ 20:1—21:45	☐ 22:1-34	☐ 23:1—24:33
32	☐ Judg 1:1-36	☐ 2:1-23	☐ 3:1-31	☐ 4:1-24	☐ 5:1-31	☐ 6:1-40	☐ 7:1-25
33	☐ 8:1-35	☐ 9:1-57	☐ 10:1—11:40	☐ 12:1—13:25	☐ 14:1—15:20	☐ 16:1-31	☐ 17:1—18:31
34	☐ 19:1-30	☐ 20:1-48	☐ 21:1-25	☐ Ruth 1:1-22	☐ 2:1-23	☐ 3:1-18	☐ 4:1-22
35	☐ 1 Sam 1:1-28	☐ 2:1-36	☐ 3:1—4:22	☐ 5:1—6:21	☐ 7:1—8:22	☐ 9:1-27	☐ 10:1—11:15
36	☐ 12:1—13:23	☐ 14:1-52	☐ 15:1-35	☐ 16:1-23	☐ 17:1-58	☐ 18:1-30	☐ 19:1-24
37	☐ 20:1-42	☐ 21:1—22:23	☐ 23:1—24:22	☐ 25:1-44	☐ 26:1-25	☐ 27:1—28:25	☐ 29:1—30:31
38	☐ 31:1-13	☐ 2 Sam 1:1-27	☐ 2:1-32	☐ 3:1-39	☐ 4:1—5:25	☐ 6:1-23	☐ 7:1-29
39	☐ 8:1—9:13	☐ 10:1—11:27	☐ 12:1-31	☐ 13:1-39	☐ 14:1-33	☐ 15:1—16:23	☐ 17:1—18:33
40	☐ 19:1-43	☐ 20:1—21:22	☐ 22:1-51	☐ 23:1-39	☐ 24:1-25	☐ 1 Kings 1:1-19	☐ 1:20-53
41	☐ 2:1-46	☐ 3:1-28	☐ 4:1-34	☐ 5:1—6:38	☐ 7:1-22	☐ 7:23-51	☐ 8:1-36
42	☐ 8:37-66	☐ 9:1-28	☐ 10:1-29	☐ 11:1-43	☐ 12:1-33	☐ 13:1-34	☐ 14:1-31
43	☐ 15:1-34	☐ 16:1—17:24	☐ 18:1-46	☐ 19:1-21	☐ 20:1-43	☐ 21:1—22:53	☐ 2 Kings 1:1-18
44	☐ 2:1—3:27	☐ 4:1-44	☐ 5:1—6:33	☐ 7:1-20	☐ 8:1-29	☐ 9:1-37	☐ 10:1-36
45	☐ 11:1—12:21	☐ 13:1—14:29	☐ 15:1-38	☐ 16:1-20	☐ 17:1-41	☐ 18:1-37	☐ 19:1-37
46	☐ 20:1—21:26	☐ 22:1-20	☐ 23:1-37	☐ 24:1—25:30	☐ 1 Chron 1:1-54	☐ 2:1—3:24	☐ 4:1—5:26
47	☐ 6:1-81	☐ 7:1-40	☐ 8:1-40	☐ 9:1-44	☐ 10:1—11:47	☐ 12:1-40	☐ 13:1—14:17
48	☐ 15:1—16:43	☐ 17:1-27	☐ 18:1—19:19	☐ 20:1—21:30	☐ 22:1—23:32	☐ 24:1—25:31	☐ 26:1-32
49	☐ 27:1-34	☐ 28:1—29:30	☐ 2 Chron 1:1-17	☐ 2:1—3:17	☐ 4:1—5:14	☐ 6:1-42	☐ 7:1—8:18
50	☐ 9:1—10:19	☐ 11:1—12:16	☐ 13:1—15:19	☐ 16:1—17:19	☐ 18:1—19:11	☐ 20:1-37	☐ 21:1—22:12
51	☐ 23:1—24:27	☐ 25:1—26:23	☐ 27:1—28:27	☐ 29:1-36	☐ 30:1—31:21	☐ 32:1-33	☐ 33:1—34:33
52	☐ 35:1—36:23	☐ Ezra 1:1-11	☐ 2:1-70	☐ 3:1—4:24	☐ 5:1—6:22	☐ 7:1-28	☐ 8:1-36

Reading Schedule for the Recovery Version of the Old Testament with Footnotes

Wk.	Lord's Day	Monday	Tuesday	Wednesday	Thursday	Friday	Saturday
53	☐ 9:1—10:44	☐ Neh 1:1-11	☐ 2:1—3:32	☐ 4:1—5:19	☐ 6:1-19	☐ 7:1-73	☐ 8:1-18
54	☐ 9:1-20	☐ 9:21-38	☐ 10:1—11:36	☐ 12:1-47	☐ 13:1-31	☐ Esth 1:1-22	☐ 2:1—3:15
55	☐ 4:1—5:14	☐ 6:1—7:10	☐ 8:1-17	☐ 9:1—10:3	☐ Job 1:1-22	☐ 2:1—3:26	☐ 4:1—5:27
56	☐ 6:1—7:21	☐ 8:1—9:35	☐ 10:1—11:20	☐ 12:1—13:28	☐ 14:1—15:35	☐ 16:1—17:16	☐ 18:1—19:29
57	☐ 20:1—21:34	☐ 22:1—23:17	☐ 24:1—25:6	☐ 26:1—27:23	☐ 28:1—29:25	☐ 30:1—31:40	☐ 32:1—33:33
58	☐ 34:1—35:16	☐ 36:1-33	☐ 37:1-24	☐ 38:1-41	☐ 39:1-30	☐ 40:1-24	☐ 41:1-34
59	☐ 42:1-17	☐ Psa 1:1-6	☐ 2:1—3:8	☐ 4:1—6:10	☐ 7:1—8:9	☐ 9:1—10:18	☐ 11:1—15:5
60	☐ 16:1—17:15	☐ 18:1-50	☐ 19:1—21:13	☐ 22:1-31	☐ 23:1—24:10	☐ 25:1—27:14	☐ 28:1—30:12
61	☐ 31:1—32:11	☐ 33:1—34:22	☐ 35:1—36:12	☐ 37:1-40	☐ 38:1—39:13	☐ 40:1—41:13	☐ 42:1—43:5
62	☐ 44:1-26	☐ 45:1-17	☐ 46:1—48:14	☐ 49:1—50:23	☐ 51:1—52:9	☐ 53:1—55:23	☐ 56:1—58:11
63	☐ 59:1—61:8	☐ 62:1—64:10	☐ 65:1—67:7	☐ 68:1-35	☐ 69:1—70:5	☐ 71:1—72:20	☐ 73:1—74:23
64	☐ 75:1—77:20	☐ 78:1-72	☐ 79:1—81:16	☐ 82:1—84:12	☐ 85:1—87:7	☐ 88:1—89:52	☐ 90:1—91:16
65	☐ 92:1—94:23	☐ 95:1—97:12	☐ 98:1—101:8	☐ 102:1—103:22	☐ 104:1—105:45	☐ 106:1-48	☐ 107:1-43
66	☐ 108:1—109:31	☐ 110:1—112:10	☐ 113:1—115:18	☐ 116:1—118:29	☐ 119:1-32	☐ 119:33-72	☐ 119:73-120
67	☐ 119:121-176	☐ 120:1—124:8	☐ 125:1—128:6	☐ 129:1—132:18	☐ 133:1—135:21	☐ 136:1—138:8	☐ 139:1—140:13
68	☐ 141:1—144:15	☐ 145:1—147:20	☐ 148:1—150:6	☐ Prov 1:1-33	☐ 2:1—3:35	☐ 4:1—5:23	☐ 6:1-35
69	☐ 7:1—8:36	☐ 9:1—10:32	☐ 11:1—12:28	☐ 13:1—14:35	☐ 15:1-33	☐ 16:1-33	☐ 17:1-28
70	☐ 18:1-24	☐ 19:1—20:30	☐ 21:1—22:29	☐ 23:1-35	☐ 24:1—25:28	☐ 26:1—27:27	☐ 28:1—29:27
71	☐ 30:1-33	☐ 31:1-31	☐ Eccl 1:1-18	☐ 2:1—3:22	☐ 4:1—5:20	☐ 6:1—7:29	☐ 8:1—9:18
72	☐ 10:1—11:10	☐ 12:1-14	☐ S.S 1:1-8	☐ 1:9-17	☐ 2:1-17	☐ 3:1-11	☐ 4:1-8
73	☐ 4:9-16	☐ 5:1-16	☐ 6:1-13	☐ 7:1-13	☐ 8:1-14	☐ Isa 1:1-11	☐ 1:12-31
74	☐ 2:1-22	☐ 3:1-26	☐ 4:1-6	☐ 5:1-30	☐ 6:1-13	☐ 7:1-25	☐ 8:1-22
75	☐ 9:1-21	☐ 10:1-34	☐ 11:1—12:6	☐ 13:1-22	☐ 14:1-14	☐ 14:15-32	☐ 15:1—16:14
76	☐ 17:1—18:7	☐ 19:1-25	☐ 20:1—21:17	☐ 22:1-25	☐ 23:1-18	☐ 24:1-23	☐ 25:1-12
77	☐ 26:1-21	☐ 27:1-13	☐ 28:1-29	☐ 29:1-24	☐ 30:1-33	☐ 31:1—32:20	☐ 33:1-24
78	☐ 34:1-17	☐ 35:1-10	☐ 36:1-22	☐ 37:1-38	☐ 38:1—39:8	☐ 40:1-31	☐ 41:1-29

Reading Schedule for the Recovery Version of the Old Testament with Footnotes

Wk.	Lord's Day	Monday	Tuesday	Wednesday	Thursday	Friday	Saturday
79	☐ 42:1-25	☐ 43:1-28	☐ 44:1-28	☐ 45:1-25	☐ 46:1-13	☐ 47:1-15	☐ 48:1-22
80	☐ 49:1-13	☐ 49:14-26	☐ 50:1—51:23	☐ 52:1-15	☐ 53:1-12	☐ 54:1-17	☐ 55:1-13
81	☐ 56:1-12	☐ 57:1-21	☐ 58:1-14	☐ 59:1-21	☐ 60:1-22	☐ 61:1-11	☐ 62:1-12
82	☐ 63:1-19	☐ 64:1-12	☐ 65:1-24	☐ 66:1-24	☐ Jer 1:1-19	☐ 2:1-19	☐ 2:20-37
83	☐ 3:1-25	☐ 4:1-31	☐ 5:1-31	☐ 6:1-30	☐ 7:1-34	☐ 8:1-22	☐ 9:1-26
84	☐ 10:1-25	☐ 11:1—12:17	☐ 13:1-27	☐ 14:1-22	☐ 15:1-21	☐ 16:1—17:27	☐ 18:1-23
85	☐ 19:1—20:18	☐ 21:1—22:30	☐ 23:1-40	☐ 24:1—25:38	☐ 26:1—27:22	☐ 28:1—29:32	☐ 30:1-24
86	☐ 31:1-23	☐ 31:24-40	☐ 32:1-44	☐ 33:1-26	☐ 34:1-22	☐ 35:1-19	☐ 36:1-32
87	☐ 37:1-21	☐ 38:1-28	☐ 39:1—40:16	☐ 41:1—42:22	☐ 43:1—44:30	☐ 45:1—46:28	☐ 47:1—48:16
88	☐ 48:17-47	☐ 49:1-22	☐ 49:23-39	☐ 50:1-27	☐ 50:28-46	☐ 51:1-27	☐ 51:28-64
89	☐ 52:1-34	☐ Lam 1:1-22	☐ 2:1-22	☐ 3:1-39	☐ 3:40-66	☐ 4:1-22	☐ 5:1-22
90	☐ Ezek 1:1-14	☐ 1:15-28	☐ 2:1—3:27	☐ 4:1—5:17	☐ 6:1—7:27	☐ 8:1—9:11	☐ 10:1—11:25
91	☐ 12:1—13:23	☐ 14:1—15:8	☐ 16:1-63	☐ 17:1—18:32	☐ 19:1-14	☐ 20:1-49	☐ 21:1-32
92	☐ 22:1-31	☐ 23:1-49	☐ 24:1-27	☐ 25:1—26:21	☐ 27:1-36	☐ 28:1-26	☐ 29:1—30:26
93	☐ 31:1—32:32	☐ 33:1-33	☐ 34:1-31	☐ 35:1—36:21	☐ 36:22-38	☐ 37:1-28	☐ 38:1—39:29
94	☐ 40:1-27	☐ 40:28-49	☐ 41:1-26	☐ 42:1—43:27	☐ 44:1-31	☐ 45:1-25	☐ 46:1-24
95	☐ 47:1-23	☐ 48:1-35	☐ Dan 1:1-21	☐ 2:1-30	☐ 2:31-49	☐ 3:1-30	☐ 4:1-37
96	☐ 5:1-31	☐ 6:1-28	☐ 7:1-12	☐ 7:13-28	☐ 8:1-27	☐ 9:1-27	☐ 10:1-21
97	☐ 11:1-22	☐ 11:23-45	☐ 12:1-13	☐ Hosea 1:1-11	☐ 2:1-23	☐ 3:1—4:19	☐ 5:1-15
98	☐ 6:1-11	☐ 7:1-16	☐ 8:1-14	☐ 9:1-17	☐ 10:1-15	☐ 11:1-12	☐ 12:1-14
99	☐ 13:1—14:9	☐ Joel 1:1-20	☐ 2:1-16	☐ 2:17-32	☐ 3:1-21	☐ Amos 1:1-15	☐ 2:1-16
100	☐ 3:1-15	☐ 4:1—5:27	☐ 6:1—7:17	☐ 8:1—9:15	☐ Obad 1-21	☐ Jonah 1:1-17	☐ 2:1—4:11
101	☐ Micah 1:1-16	☐ 2:1—3:12	☐ 4:1—5:15	☐ 6:1—7:20	☐ Nahum 1:1-15	☐ 2:1—3:19	☐ Hab 1:1-17
102	☐ 2:1-20	☐ 3:1-19	☐ Zeph 1:1-18	☐ 2:1-15	☐ 3:1-20	☐ Hag 1:1-15	☐ 2:1-23
103	☐ Zech 1:1-21	☐ 2:1-13	☐ 3:1-10	☐ 4:1-14	☐ 5:1—6:15	☐ 7:1—8:23	☐ 9:1-17
104	☐ 10:1—11:17	☐ 12:1—13:9	☐ 14:1-21	☐ Mal 1:1-14	☐ 2:1-17	☐ 3:1-18	☐ 4:1-6

Reading Schedule for the Recovery Version of the New Testament with Footnotes

Wk.	Lord's Day	Monday	Tuesday	Wednesday	Thursday	Friday	Saturday
1	☐ Matt 1:1-2	☐ 1:3-7	☐ 1:8-17	☐ 1:18-25	☐ 2:1-23	☐ 3:1-6	3:7-17
2	☐ 4:1-11	☐ 4:12-25	☐ 5:1-4	☐ 5:5-12	☐ 5:13-20	☐ 5:21-26	5:27-48
3	☐ 6:1-8	☐ 6:9-18	☐ 6:19-34	☐ 7:1-12	☐ 7:13-29	☐ 8:1-13	8:14-22
4	☐ 8:23-34	☐ 9:1-13	☐ 9:14-17	☐ 9:18-34	☐ 9:35—10:5	☐ 10:6-25	10:26-42
5	☐ 11:1-15	☐ 11:16-30	☐ 12:1-14	☐ 12:15-32	☐ 12:33-42	☐ 12:43—13:2	13:3-12
6	☐ 13:13-30	☐ 13:31-43	☐ 13:44-58	☐ 14:1-13	☐ 14:14-21	☐ 14:22-36	15:1-20
7	☐ 15:21-31	☐ 15:32-39	☐ 16:1-12	☐ 16:13-20	☐ 16:21-28	☐ 17:1-13	17:14-27
8	☐ 18:1-14	☐ 18:15-22	☐ 18:23-35	☐ 19:1-15	☐ 19:16-30	☐ 20:1-16	20:17-34
9	☐ 21:1-11	☐ 21:12-22	☐ 21:23-32	☐ 21:33-46	☐ 22:1-22	☐ 22:23-33	22:34-46
10	☐ 23:1-12	☐ 23:13-39	☐ 24:1-14	☐ 24:15-31	☐ 24:32-51	☐ 25:1-13	25:14-30
11	☐ 25:31-46	☐ 26:1-16	☐ 26:17-35	☐ 26:36-46	☐ 26:47-64	☐ 26:65-75	27:1-26
12	☐ 27:27-44	☐ 27:45-56	☐ 27:57—28:15	☐ 28:16-20	☐ Mark 1:1	☐ 1:2-6	1:7-13
13	☐ 1:14-28	☐ 1:29-45	☐ 2:1-12	☐ 2:13-28	☐ 3:1-19	☐ 3:20-35	4:1-25
14	☐ 4:26-41	☐ 5:1-20	☐ 5:21-43	☐ 6:1-29	☐ 6:30-56	☐ 7:1-23	7:24-37
15	☐ 8:1-26	☐ 8:27—9:1	☐ 9:2-29	☐ 9:30-50	☐ 10:1-16	☐ 10:17-34	10:35-52
16	☐ 11:1-16	☐ 11:17-33	☐ 12:1-27	☐ 12:28-44	☐ 13:1-13	☐ 13:14-37	14:1-26
17	☐ 14:27-52	☐ 14:53-72	☐ 15:1-15	☐ 15:16-47	☐ 16:1-8	☐ 16:9-20	Luke 1:1-4
18	☐ 1:5-25	☐ 1:26-46	☐ 1:47-56	☐ 1:57-80	☐ 2:1-8	☐ 2:9-20	2:21-39
19	☐ 2:40-52	☐ 3:1-20	☐ 3:21-38	☐ 4:1-13	☐ 4:14-30	☐ 4:31-44	5:1-26
20	☐ 5:27—6:16	☐ 6:17-38	☐ 6:39-49	☐ 7:1-17	☐ 7:18-23	☐ 7:24-35	7:36-50
21	☐ 8:1-15	☐ 8:16-25	☐ 8:26-39	☐ 8:40-56	☐ 9:1-17	☐ 9:18-26	9:27-36
22	☐ 9:37-50	☐ 9:51-62	☐ 10:1-11	☐ 10:12-24	☐ 10:25-37	☐ 10:38-42	11:1-13
23	☐ 11:14-26	☐ 11:27-36	☐ 11:37-54	☐ 12:1-12	☐ 12:13-21	☐ 12:22-34	12:35-48
24	☐ 12:49-59	☐ 13:1-9	☐ 13:10-17	☐ 13:18-30	☐ 13:31—14:6	☐ 14:7-14	14:15-24
25	☐ 14:25-35	☐ 15:1-10	☐ 15:11-21	☐ 15:22-32	☐ 16:1-13	☐ 16:14-22	16:23-31
26	☐ 17:1-19	☐ 17:20-37	☐ 18:1-14	☐ 18:15-30	☐ 18:31-43	☐ 19:1-10	19:11-27

Reading Schedule for the Recovery Version of the New Testament with Footnotes

Wk.	Lord's Day	Monday	Tuesday	Wednesday	Thursday	Friday	Saturday
27	☐ Luke 19:28-48	☐ 20:1-19	☐ 20:20-38	☐ 20:39—21:4	☐ 21:5-27	☐ 21:28-38	☐ 22:1-20
28	☐ 22:21-38	☐ 22:39-54	☐ 22:55-71	☐ 23:1-43	☐ 23:44-56	☐ 24:1-12	☐ 24:13-35
29	☐ 24:36-53	☐ John 1:1-13	☐ 1:14-18	☐ 1:19-34	☐ 1:35-51	☐ 2:1-11	☐ 2:12-22
30	☐ 2:23—3:13	☐ 3:14-21	☐ 3:22-36	☐ 4:1-14	☐ 4:15-26	☐ 4:27-42	☐ 4:43-54
31	☐ 5:1-16	☐ 5:17-30	☐ 5:31-47	☐ 6:1-15	☐ 6:16-31	☐ 6:32-51	☐ 6:52-71
32	☐ 7:1-9	☐ 7:10-24	☐ 7:25-36	☐ 7:37-52	☐ 7:53—8:11	☐ 8:12-27	☐ 8:28-44
33	☐ 8:45-59	☐ 9:1-13	☐ 9:14-34	☐ 9:35—10:9	☐ 10:10-30	☐ 10:31—11:4	☐ 11:5-22
34	☐ 11:23-40	☐ 11:41-57	☐ 12:1-11	☐ 12:12-24	☐ 12:25-36	☐ 12:37-50	☐ 13:1-11
35	☐ 13:12-30	☐ 13:31-38	☐ 14:1-6	☐ 14:7-20	☐ 14:21-31	☐ 15:1-11	☐ 15:12-27
36	☐ 16:1-15	☐ 16:16-33	☐ 17:1-5	☐ 17:6-13	☐ 17:14-24	☐ 17:25—18:11	☐ 18:12-27
37	☐ 18:28-40	☐ 19:1-16	☐ 19:17-30	☐ 19:31-42	☐ 20:1-13	☐ 20:14-18	☐ 20:19-22
38	☐ 20:23-31	☐ 21:1-14	☐ 21:15-22	☐ 21:23-25	☐ Acts 1:1-8	☐ 1:9-14	☐ 1:15-26
39	☐ 2:1-13	☐ 2:14-21	☐ 2:22-36	☐ 2:37-41	☐ 2:42-47	☐ 3:1-18	☐ 3:19—4:22
40	☐ 4:23-37	☐ 5:1-16	☐ 5:17-32	☐ 5:33-42	☐ 6:1—7:1	☐ 7:2-29	☐ 7:30-60
41	☐ 8:1-13	☐ 8:14-25	☐ 8:26-40	☐ 9:1-19	☐ 9:20-43	☐ 10:1-16	☐ 10:17-33
42	☐ 10:34-48	☐ 11:1-18	☐ 11:19-30	☐ 12:1-25	☐ 13:1-12	☐ 13:13-43	☐ 13:44—14:5
43	☐ 14:6-28	☐ 15:1-12	☐ 15:13-34	☐ 15:35—16:5	☐ 16:6-18	☐ 16:19-40	☐ 17:1-18
44	☐ 17:19-34	☐ 18:1-17	☐ 18:18-28	☐ 19:1-20	☐ 19:21-41	☐ 20:1-12	☐ 20:13-38
45	☐ 21:1-14	☐ 21:15-26	☐ 21:27-40	☐ 22:1-21	☐ 22:22-29	☐ 22:30—23:11	☐ 23:12-15
46	☐ 23:16-30	☐ 23:31—24:21	☐ 24:22—25:5	☐ 25:6-27	☐ 26:1-13	☐ 26:14-32	☐ 27:1-26
47	☐ 27:27—28:10	☐ 28:11-22	☐ 28:23-31	☐ Rom 1:1-2	☐ 1:3-7	☐ 1:8-17	☐ 1:18-25
48	☐ 1:26—2:10	☐ 2:11-29	☐ 3:1-20	☐ 3:21-31	☐ 4:1-12	☐ 4:13-25	☐ 5:1-11
49	☐ 5:12-17	☐ 5:18—6:5	☐ 6:6-11	☐ 6:12-23	☐ 7:1-12	☐ 7:13-25	☐ 8:1-2
50	☐ 8:3-6	☐ 8:7-13	☐ 8:14-25	☐ 8:26-39	☐ 9:1-18	☐ 9:19—10:3	☐ 10:4-15
51	☐ 10:16—11:10	☐ 11:11-22	☐ 11:23-36	☐ 12:1-3	☐ 12:4-21	☐ 13:1-14	☐ 14:1-12
52	☐ 14:13-23	☐ 15:1-13	☐ 15:14-33	☐ 16:1-5	☐ 16:6-24	☐ 16:25-27	☐ 1 Cor 1:1-4

Reading Schedule for the Recovery Version of the New Testament with Footnotes

Wk.	Lord's Day	Monday	Tuesday	Wednesday	Thursday	Friday	Saturday
53	☐ 1 Cor 1:5-9	☐ 1:10-17	☐ 1:18-31	☐ 2:1-5	☐ 2:6-10	☐ 2:11-16	☐ 3:1-9
54	☐ 3:10-13	☐ 3:14-23	☐ 4:1-9	☐ 4:10-21	☐ 5:1-13	☐ 6:1-11	☐ 6:12-20
55	☐ 7:1-16	☐ 7:17-24	☐ 7:25-40	☐ 8:1-13	☐ 9:1-15	☐ 9:16-27	☐ 10:1-4
56	☐ 10:5-13	☐ 10:14-33	☐ 11:1-6	☐ 11:7-16	☐ 11:17-26	☐ 11:27-34	☐ 12:1-11
57	☐ 12:12-22	☐ 12:23-31	☐ 13:1-13	☐ 14:1-12	☐ 14:13-25	☐ 14:26-33	☐ 14:34-40
58	☐ 15:1-19	☐ 15:20-28	☐ 15:29-34	☐ 15:35-49	☐ 15:50-58	☐ 16:1-9	☐ 16:10-24
59	☐ 2 Cor 1:1-4	☐ 1:5-14	☐ 1:15-22	☐ 1:23—2:11	☐ 2:12-17	☐ 3:1-6	☐ 3:7-11
60	☐ 3:12-18	☐ 4:1-6	☐ 4:7-12	☐ 4:13-18	☐ 5:1-8	☐ 5:9-15	☐ 5:16-21
61	☐ 6:1-13	☐ 6:14—7:4	☐ 7:5-16	☐ 8:1-15	☐ 8:16-24	☐ 9:1-15	☐ 10:1-6
62	☐ 10:7-18	☐ 11:1-15	☐ 11:16-33	☐ 12:1-10	☐ 12:11-21	☐ 13:1-10	☐ 13:11-14
63	☐ Gal 1:1-5	☐ 1:6-14	☐ 1:15-24	☐ 2:1-13	☐ 2:14-21	☐ 3:1-4	☐ 3:5-14
64	☐ 3:15-22	☐ 3:23-29	☐ 4:1-7	☐ 4:8-20	☐ 4:21-31	☐ 5:1-12	☐ 5:13-21
65	☐ 5:22-26	☐ 6:1-10	☐ 6:11-15	☐ 6:16-18	☐ Eph 1:1-3	☐ 1:4-6	☐ 1:7-10
66	☐ 1:11-14	☐ 1:15-18	☐ 1:19-23	☐ 2:1-5	☐ 2:6-10	☐ 2:11-14	☐ 2:15-18
67	☐ 2:19-22	☐ 3:1-7	☐ 3:8-13	☐ 3:14-18	☐ 3:19-21	☐ 4:1-4	☐ 4:5-10
68	☐ 4:11-16	☐ 4:17-24	☐ 4:25-32	☐ 5:1-10	☐ 5:11-21	☐ 5:22-26	☐ 5:27-33
69	☐ 6:1-9	☐ 6:10-14	☐ 6:15-18	☐ 6:19-24	☐ Phil 1:1-7	☐ 1:8-18	☐ 1:19-26
70	☐ 1:27—2:4	☐ 2:5-11	☐ 2:12-16	☐ 2:17-30	☐ 3:1-6`	☐ 3:7-11	☐ 3:12-16
71	☐ 3:17-21	☐ 4:1-9	☐ 4:10-23	☐ Col 1:1-8	☐ 1:9-13	☐ 1:14-23	☐ 1:24-29
72	☐ 2:1-7	☐ 2:8-15	☐ 2:16-23	☐ 3:1-4	☐ 3:5-15	☐ 3:16-25	☐ 4:1-18
73	☐ 1 Thes 1:1-3	☐ 1:4-10	☐ 2:1-12	☐ 2:13—3:5	☐ 3:6-13	☐ 4:1-10	☐ 4:11—5:11
74	☐ 5:12-28	☐ 2 Thes 1:1-12	☐ 2:1-17	☐ 3:1-18	☐ 1 Tim 1:1-2	☐ 1:3-4	☐ 1:5-14
75	☐ 1:15-20	☐ 2:1-7	☐ 2:8-15	☐ 3:1-13	☐ 3:14—4:5	☐ 4:6-16	☐ 5:1-25
76	☐ 6:1-10	☐ 6:11-21	☐ 2 Tim 1:1-10	☐ 1:11-18	☐ 2:1-15	☐ 2:16-26	☐ 3:1-13
77	☐ 3:14—4:8	☐ 4:9-22	☐ Titus 1:1-4	☐ 1:5-16	☐ 2:1-15	☐ 3:1-8	☐ 3:9-15
78	☐ Philem 1:1-11	☐ 1:12-25	☐ Heb 1:1-2	☐ 1:3-5	☐ 1:6-14	☐ 2:1-9	☐ 2:10-18

Reading Schedule for the Recovery Version of the New Testament with Footnotes

Wk.	Lord's Day	Monday	Tuesday	Wednesday	Thursday	Friday	Saturday
79	☐ Heb 3:1-6	☐ 3:7-19	☐ 4:1-9	☐ 4:10-13	☐ 4:14-16	☐ 5:1-10	☐ 5:11—6:3
80	☐ 6:4-8	☐ 6:9-20	☐ 7:1-10	☐ 7:11-28	☐ 8:1-6	☐ 8:7-13	☐ 9:1-4
81	☐ 9:5-14	☐ 9:15-28	☐ 10:1-18	☐ 10:19-28	☐ 10:29-39	☐ 11:1-6	☐ 11:7-19
82	☐ 11:20-31	☐ 11:32-40	☐ 12:1-2	☐ 12:3-13	☐ 12:14-17	☐ 12:18-26	☐ 12:27-29
83	☐ 13:1-7	☐ 13:8-12	☐ 13:13-15	☐ 13:16-25	☐ James 1:1-8	☐ 1:9-18	☐ 1:19-27
84	☐ 2:1-13	☐ 2:14-26	☐ 3:1-18	☐ 4:1-10	☐ 4:11-17	☐ 5:1-12	☐ 5:13-20
85	☐ 1 Pet 1:1-2	☐ 1:3-4	☐ 1:5	☐ 1:6-9	☐ 1:10-12	☐ 1:13-17	☐ 1:18-25
86	☐ 2:1-3	☐ 2:4-8	☐ 2:9-17	☐ 2:18-25	☐ 3:1-13	☐ 3:14-22	☐ 4:1-6
87	☐ 4:7-16	☐ 4:17-19	☐ 5:1-4	☐ 5:5-9	☐ 5:10-14	☐ 2 Pet 1:1-2	☐ 1:3-4
88	☐ 1:5-8	☐ 1:9-11	☐ 1:12-18	☐ 1:19-21	☐ 2:1-3	☐ 2:4-11	☐ 2:12-22
89	☐ 3:1-6	☐ 3:7-9	☐ 3:10-12	☐ 3:13-15	☐ 3:16	☐ 3:17-18	☐ 1 John 1:1-2
90	☐ 1:3-4	☐ 1:5	☐ 1:6	☐ 1:7	☐ 1:8-10	☐ 2:1-2	☐ 2:3-11
91	☐ 2:12-14	☐ 2:15-19	☐ 2:20-23	☐ 2:24-27	☐ 2:28-29	☐ 3:1-5	☐ 3:6-10
92	☐ 3:11-18	☐ 3:19-24	☐ 4:1-6	☐ 4:7-11	☐ 4:12-15	☐ 4:16—5:3	☐ 5:4-13
93	☐ 5:14-17	☐ 5:18-21	☐ 2 John 1:1-3	☐ 1:4-9	☐ 1:10-13	☐ 3 John 1:1-6	☐ 1:7-14
94	☐ Jude 1:1-4	☐ 1:5-10	☐ 1:11-19	☐ 1:20-25	☐ Rev 1:1-3	☐ 1:4-6	☐ 1:7-11
95	☐ 1:12-13	☐ 1:14-16	☐ 1:17-20	☐ 2:1-6	☐ 2:7	☐ 2:8-9	☐ 2:10-11
96	☐ 2:12-14	☐ 2:15-17	☐ 2:18-23	☐ 2:24-29	☐ 3:1-3	☐ 3:4-6	☐ 3:7-9
97	☐ 3:10-13	☐ 3:14-18	☐ 3:19-22	☐ 4:1-5	☐ 4:6-7	☐ 4:8-11	☐ 5:1-6
98	☐ 5:7-14	☐ 6:1-8	☐ 6:9-17	☐ 7:1-8	☐ 7:9-17	☐ 8:1-6	☐ 8:7-12
99	☐ 8:13—9:11	☐ 9:12-21	☐ 10:1-4	☐ 10:5-11	☐ 11:1-4	☐ 11:5-14	☐ 11:15-19
100	☐ 12:1-4	☐ 12:5-9	☐ 12:10-18	☐ 13:1-10	☐ 13:11-18	☐ 14:1-5	☐ 14:6-12
101	☐ 14:13-20	☐ 15:1-8	☐ 16:1-12	☐ 16:13-21	☐ 17:1-6	☐ 17:7-18	☐ 18:1-8
102	☐ 18:9—19:4	☐ 19:5-10	☐ 19:11-16	☐ 19:17-21	☐ 20:1-6	☐ 20:7-10	☐ 20:11-15
103	☐ 21:1	☐ 21:2	☐ 21:3-8	☐ 21:9-13	☐ 21:14-18	☐ 21:19-21	☐ 21:22-27
104	☐ 22:1	☐ 22:2	☐ 22:3-11	☐ 22:12-15	☐ 22:16-17	☐ 22:18-21	

Acts 1:21-22 ...Of the men who accompanied us all the time in which the Lord Jesus went in and went out among us, beginning from the baptism of John until the day on which He was taken up from us, one of these should become a witness of His resurrection with us.

4:33 And with great power the apostles gave testimony of the resurrection of the Lord Jesus, and great grace was upon them all.

_____
Date

Week 1 — Day 1   **Today's verses**

Acts 28:30-31 And [Paul] remained two whole years in *his* own rented dwelling and welcomed all those who came to him, proclaiming the kingdom of God and teaching the things concerning the Lord Jesus Christ with all boldness, unhindered.

John 12:24 Truly, truly, I say to you, Unless the grain of wheat falls into the ground and dies, it abides alone; but if it dies, it bears much fruit.

Acts 13:33 That God has fully fulfilled this *promise* to us their children in raising up Jesus, as it is also written in the second Psalm, "You are My Son; this day have I begotten You."

Rom. 6:9 Knowing that Christ, having been raised from the dead, dies no more; death lords it over Him no more.

_____
Date

Week 1 — Day 2   **Today's verses**

Luke 24:49 And behold, I send forth the promise of My Father upon you; but as for you, stay in the city until you put on power from on high.

Acts 1:14 These all continued steadfastly with one accord in prayer...

2:46 And day by day, continuing steadfastly with one accord in the temple and breaking bread from house to house...

_____
Date

Eph. 1:19-20 And what is the surpassing greatness of His power toward us who believe, according to the operation of the might of His strength, which He caused to operate in Christ in raising Him from the dead...

Matt. 18:19 ...If two of you are in harmony on earth concerning any matter for which they ask, it will be done for them from My Father who is in the heavens.

_____
Date

Week 1 — Day 3   **Today's verses**

Acts 1:8 But you shall receive power when the Holy Spirit comes upon you, and you shall be My witnesses both in Jerusalem and in all Judea and Samaria and unto the uttermost part of the earth.

2:32 This Jesus God has raised up, of which we all are witnesses.

_____
Date

Week 2 — Day 1

Phil. 1:27 Only, conduct yourselves in a manner worthy of the gospel of Christ, that...I may hear of the things concerning you, that you stand firm in one spirit, with one soul striving together *along* with the faith of the gospel.

2:2 Make my joy full, that you think the same thing, having the same love, joined in soul, thinking the one thing.

Rom. 15:6 That with one accord you may with one mouth glorify the God and Father of our Lord Jesus Christ.

Date

Jer. 32:39 And I will give them one heart and one way, to fear Me all the days, for their own good and for *the good of* their children after them.

Mark 12:30 "And you shall love the Lord your God from your whole heart and from your whole soul and from your whole mind and from your whole strength."

John 14:6 Jesus said to him, I am the way...

Date

---

1 Cor. 11:16 ...If anyone seems to be contentious, we do not have such a custom *of being so,* neither the churches of God.

Phil. 2:1-2 If there is therefore any encouragement in Christ, if any consolation of love, if any fellowship of spirit, if any tenderheartedness and compassions, make my joy full, that you think the same thing, having the same love, joined in soul, thinking the one thing.

Date

Week 2 — Day 1   Today's verses

Acts 1:14 These all continued steadfastly with one accord in prayer...

2:46 And day by day, continuing steadfastly with one accord in the temple and breaking bread from house to house...

4:24 And when they heard *this,* they lifted up *their* voice with one accord to God...

Date

Week 2 — Day 2   Today's verses

Eph. 1:3 Blessed be the God and Father of our Lord Jesus Christ, who has blessed us with every spiritual blessing in the heavenlies in Christ.

1 Cor. 12:12 For even as the body is one and has many members, yet all the members of the body, being many, are one body, so also is the Christ.

Date

Week 2 — Day 3   Today's verses

Matt. 18:19 ...If two of you are in harmony on earth concerning any matter for which they ask, it will be done for them....

Acts 2:42 And they continued steadfastly in the teaching and the fellowship of the apostles, in the breaking of bread and the prayers.

1 Cor. 4:17 ...Even as I teach everywhere in every church.

Date

Week 3 — Day 1

Matt. 3:11 ...He Himself will baptize you in the Holy Spirit and fire.

Acts 2:2 And suddenly there was a sound out of heaven, as of a rushing violent wind, and it filled the whole house where they were sitting.

4 And they were all filled with the Holy Spirit and began to speak in different tongues...

Today's verses

Matt. 1:18 Now the origin of Jesus Christ was in this way: His mother, Mary, after she had been engaged to Joseph, before they came together, was found to be with child of the Holy Spirit.

20 ...That which has been begotten in her [Mary] is of the Holy Spirit.

Luke 4:18 "The Spirit of the Lord is upon Me, because He has anointed Me...; He has sent Me..."

_____
Date

Week 3 — Day 2

Acts 11:15 And as I began to speak, the Holy Spirit fell on them just as also on us in the beginning.

17 If therefore God has given to them the equal gift as also to us who have believed on the Lord Jesus Christ, who was I that I could have forbidden God?

13:9 But Saul...filled with the Holy Spirit...

Today's verses

John 20:22 And when He had said this, He breathed into them and said to them, Receive the Holy Spirit.

Luke 24:49 And behold, I send forth the promise of My Father upon you; but as for you, stay in the city until you put on power from on high.

1 Cor. 12:13 For also in one Spirit we were all baptized into one Body...and were all given to drink one Spirit.

_____
Date

Week 3 — Day 3

Acts 2:32-33 This Jesus God has raised up, of which we all are witnesses. Therefore having been exalted to the right hand of God and having received the promise of the Holy Spirit from the Father, He has poured out this which you both see and hear.

Eph. 1:22 And He...gave Him to be Head over all things to the church.

Acts 4:8 Then Peter, filled with the Holy Spirit...

Today's verses

John 6:57 As...I live because of the Father, so he who eats Me, he also shall live because of Me.

Acts 1:5 For John baptized with water, but you shall be baptized in the Holy Spirit not many days from now.

8 But you shall receive power when the Holy Spirit comes upon you, and you shall be My witnesses...

_____
Date

Acts 2:42 And they continued steadfastly in the teaching and the fellowship of the apostles, in the breaking of bread and the prayers.

8:17 Then they [the apostles] laid their hands on them, and they received the Holy Spirit.

1 John 1:2-3 [And the life was manifested, and we have seen and testify and report to you the eternal life, which was with the Father and was manifested to us); that which we have seen and heard we report also to you that you also may have fellowship with us, and indeed our fellowship is with the Father and with His Son Jesus Christ.

Ezek. 1:5-6 ...And this was [the four living creatures'] appearance: They had the likeness of a man. And every one had four faces, and every one of them had four wings.

9 Their wings were joined one to another; they did not turn as they went; each went straight forward.

12 ...Wherever the Spirit was to go, they went; they did not turn as they went.

Week 4 — Day 1   Today's verses

Heb. 1:1-2 God, having spoken of old in many portions and in many ways to the fathers in the prophets, has at the last of these days spoken to us in the Son....

Acts 2:42 And they continued steadfastly in the teaching and the fellowship of the apostles....

_____
Date

Week 4 — Day 2   Today's verses

John 1:14 And the Word became flesh and tabernacled among us...

1 Cor. 15:45 ...The last Adam *became* a life-giving Spirit.

Rev. 5:6-7 And I saw...a Lamb standing as having *just* been slain...And He came and took *the scroll* out of the right hand of Him who sits upon the throne.

_____
Date

Week 4 — Day 3   Today's verses

1 Tim. 1:3-4 Even as I exhorted you...to remain in Ephesus in order that you might charge certain ones not to teach different things nor to give heed to myths and unending genealogies, which produce questionings rather than God's economy, which is in faith.

2 Tim. 1:15 This you know, that all who are in Asia turned away from me...

_____
Date

Today's verses

Phil. 3:7-8 But what things were gains to me, these I have counted as loss on account of Christ. But moreover I also count all things to be loss on account of the excellency of the knowledge of Christ Jesus my Lord ...that I may gain Christ.

Gal. 1:15-16 But when it pleased God, who set me apart from my mother's womb and called me through His grace, to reveal His Son in me that I might announce Him as the gospel among the Gentiles...

Col. 1:25-26 ...I became a minister according to the stewardship of God, which was given to me for you, to complete the word of God, the mystery...

_____
Date

Today's verses

Acts 9:3-4 ...Suddenly a light from heaven flashed around him. And he fell on the ground and heard a voice...

8-9 And Saul rose from the ground; and though his eyes were open, he could see nothing. And they led him by the hand... And he was three days without seeing, and he neither ate nor drank.

Acts 9:15 ...This man is a chosen vessel to Me, to bear My name before both the Gentiles and kings and the sons of Israel.

Rom. 9:23 In order that He might make known the riches of His glory upon vessels of mercy, which He had before prepared unto glory.

Eph. 3:19 ...That you may be filled unto all the fullness of God.

_____
Date

Today's verses

Acts 9:4-6 ...Saul, Saul, why are you persecuting Me? And he said, Who are You, Lord? And He said, I am Jesus, whom you persecute. But rise up and enter into the city, and it will be told to you what you must do.

17 ...And laying his hands on him, he said, Saul, brother, the Lord has sent me...so that you may receive your sight and be filled with the Holy Spirit.

Acts 26:16 ...I have appeared to you for this purpose, to appoint you as a minister and a witness both of the things in which you have seen Me and of the things in which I will appear to you.

19 Therefore, King Agrippa, I was not disobedient to the heavenly vision.

_____
Date

Week 6 — Day 1

Acts 2:32-33 This Jesus God has raised up, of which we all are witnesses. Therefore having been exalted to the right hand of God and having received the promise of the Holy Spirit from the Father, He has poured out this which you both see and hear.

36 ...God has made Him both Lord and Christ, this Jesus whom you have crucified.

Today's verses

Acts 3:14-15 But you denied the holy and righteous One and asked that a man *who was* a murderer be granted to you; and the Author of life you killed, whom God has raised from the dead, of which we are witnesses.

Date

Week 6 — Day 2

Acts 9:20 And immediately he [Saul] proclaimed Jesus in the synagogues, that this One is the Son of God.

22 ...And he [Saul] confounded the Jews dwelling in Damascus by proving that this One is the Christ.

John 20:31 But these have been written that you may believe that Jesus is the Christ, the Son of God, and that believing, you may have life in His name.

Today's verses

Acts 4:11-12 This is the stone which was considered as nothing by you, the builders, which has become the head of the corner. And there is salvation in no other, for neither is there another name under heaven given among men in which we must be saved.

Date

Week 6 — Day 3

Acts 2:23-24 This man, delivered up by the determined counsel and foreknowledge of God, you, through the hand of lawless men, nailed to a *cross* and killed; whom God has raised up, having loosed the pangs of death, since it was not possible for Him to be held by it.

Today's verses

Acts 13:33-34 That God has fully fulfilled this *promise* to us their children in raising up Jesus, as it is also written in the second Psalm, "You are My Son; this day have I begotten You." And as to His having raised Him up from the dead, no longer to return to corruption, He spoke in this way, "I will give you the holy things of David, the faithful things."

Date